# HINDU
## Feasts Fasts
## &
## Ceremonies

# HINDU
## Feasts Fasts
## &
## Ceremonies

Dr. Jayshree Sarkar

Srishti
PUBLISHERS & DISTRIBUTORS

Srishti Publishers & Distributors
64-A, Adhchini
Sri Aurobindo Marg
New Delhi 110017

First published by Srishti Publishers & Distributors 1999
Second Impression 2000
Reprinted 2003
Copyright © Srishti Publishers & Distributors 1999
Copyright © Dr. Jayshree Sarkar 1999
ISBN 81-87075-15-5
Rs. 125.00

Cover Design by Arrt Creations
45 Nehru Apartment, New Delhi 110019

Printed and bound in India by
Saurabh Print-O-Pack, Noida

All rights reserved. No part of this publication may be
reproduced, stored in a retrieval system, or transmitted, in
any form or by any means, electronic, mechanical,
photocopying, recording, or other wise, without the prior
written permission of the Publisher.

# Contents

# *Introduction*

The folklore of a country is never so well known even by the 'folk' of the country itself, that popular literature concerning it is not to be heartily welcomed. Moreover there is always a young generation growing up which is waiting to be instructed in it by the easiest and widest possible means.

The simpler tenets of religion and the more popular tales and legends are learned from the lips of parents and teachers: but there is much that can only be learned from books. Further, in these days of hurry and stress, by which even India is being more or less affected, the old leisurely, yet possibly more thorough, methods of oral tradition and teaching are no longer possible, and we must trust more and more to written and printed records. This book is an excellent work in collecting, arranging and recording in concise and easily assimilable formsome of the more noticeable tales, traditions, customs, beliefs, and ceremonies of the Hindus. For there are mines of wealth to be exploited in this manner, and there is work for many scores of writers, compilers and translators.

There is no country in the world, moreover, where such studies are of more importance than in India, for with the Hindu, customs and traditions explain almost every act of his everyday life. As a learned writer on the Hindus has well said:-
"With the Hindu, religion is not a thing for times and seasons only, but professes to regulate his life in its many relations. It

orders ceremonies to be performed on his behalf before he is born, and others after his death. It ordains those attendant on his birth, his early training, his food, his style of dress and its manufacture, his employment, marriage, amusements. It seeks to regulate not only his private life, but also his domestic and national life. To treat of the ordinary life of the Hindu is to describe his religion."

At the same time there is one point that must ever be kept in mind, namely the danger of generalising with regard to Hindu manners, customs, ceremonies and traditions. As the writer quoted above remarks:- "It should be remembered that descriptions true of certain classes or of certain districts may not be correct of other classes or other districts; and that frequently the residents of one district are totally ignorant of what prevails in others. This can scarcely be wondered at when we consider the number of books which are accepted by the people as divinely given for authorities concerning the gods and religious life. The people of one district are familiar with only a small part of one book, whilst those of other districts found their faiths on other books or different parts of the same. In addition to this, it must not be forgotten that a century ago there was no prose literature, no newspapers, magazines, or novels; whilst the theatrical representations were almost entirely confined to mythological subjects. It is no uncommon thing to find a custom at home, or a ceremony in worship, supported by quite different authorities by different people."

It seems hardly necessary to point out or emphasise how

specially valuable to foreign students are these works, and others similar to them. The bounden duty laid upon all Europeans living in this country and earning their livelihood in it, of striving to understand and appreciate the people among whom they dwell, needs no argument or demonstration. Such knowledge and appreciation cannot be acquired without careful study and observation. But nowadays, at any rate, he who wishes may read many excellent treatises both by natives of India and by Europeans on various aspects and characteristics of Hinduism and the Hindus; and for a general workaday knowledge of the Hindus there is no more useful, and at the same time more interesting, study than that of current beliefs and practices such as are described in this little volume.

# The Mahalaya Amavasa

Amavasa, or the day of the conjunction of the sun and the moon, occurs once every month and it is a day considered by the Hindus to be specially set apart for the offering of oblations and the performance of religious cermonies to the Pitris or the spirits of departed ancestors. Such being the general belibef, what is the reason for the Hindus paying greater attention to the Mahalaya Amavasa, or the new moon day of the month of *Kanya* (Tamil Purattasi) when the sun is in the sign *Virgo*? The Itihasa, a great authority on the religious rites of the Hindus, says that the moment the sun enters the sign *Virgo (Kanya)* the departed spirits, leaving their abode in the world of Yama, the Destroyer, come down to the world of man and occupy the houses of their descendants in this world or as it is said in Sanskrit, *Kanya yate surye pitaras tishtanti sve grihe.* Therefore the fortnight preceding the new moon of the month of *Kanya* is considered as the fortnight which is specially sacred to the propitiation of the *Manes* or departed spirits. *Dine dine gaya tulyam* - The ceremonies in honour of the *Manes* performed during each day of this fortnight are considerd to be equal to the ceremonies performed in the sacerd city of Gaya. But instead of performing these rites on each of the days of the fortnight, most Hindus do so only on one of the days. Orthodox Hindus, however, perform ceremonies on every one of the days of this fortnight. These ceremonies terminate on the Mahalaya Amavasa day, which is therefore observed with greater sanctity than other new moon days. If, through unavoidable causes, any Hindu is not able to perform his Mahalaya rites during the course of the fortnight preceding the Mahalaya Amavasa, he is allowed as a concession to perform the same in the fortnight succeeding this new moon, because it is said that the Manes continue to linger in his house, expecting him to perform the ceremonies, till the sun enters the sign *Scorpio (Vichchhika), i.e.* till about the next full moon day. If even by that time a Hindu has not performed these ceremonies to the Manes they are said to become disgustesd with him and return to the world of Yama after cursing their descendants in this world. *Vrichchhika darsanat yanti nirasa pitaro gatah.*

Such is the belief about the Mahalaya Amavasa and the two lunar fortnights which precede and succeed it. The month of *Kanya* is thus reserved for the worhsip of departed spirits and the most propitious portion of the month for such worship is the fortnight preceding the Mahalaya Amavasa. Generally speaking, every Hindu strictly observes his Mahalaya. If he is careless about it, he will find it difficult to have a peaceful time with the old ladies in his house.

# The Ardra

The followers of the Saiva religion deem five places in southern India most holy, and they are:- Conjeeveram, where Shiva is worshipped in the shape of *prithivi-linga* or as the representative of the element earth; Tiruvanaikovil, near Trichinopoly, where he is worshipped in the shape of water-*linga;* sri kalahasti, the shrine contining the air *linga;* Tiruvannamalai, the seat of the fire-*linga;* and Chidambaram, the abode of the ether. The several forms of god Shiva in these sacerd shrines are considered to be the bodies or casements of the soul whose natural bases are the five elements – earth, water, fire, air, and ether. The apprehension of God in the last of these five as ether is, according to the Shiva school of philosophy, the highest form of worship, for ,it is not the worship of God in a tangible form, but the worship of what, to ordinary minds, is vacuum, which nevertheless lead to the attainment of a Knowledge leads of the all-pervading without physical accessories in the shape of any linga,which is after all,an emblem. That this is the case at Chidambaram is known to every Hindu, for if he ever asks the priests to show him the God in the temple he is pointed to an empty space in the most holy of the holies, which has been termed the *Akasa*, or ether-*linga*. In this lies the so-called *Chidambara-rashya* – the secret of worship in the sacred city of Chidambaram. When any devotee has reached the stage of worshipping God in this manner, he is, according to the Saiva doctrine, deemed to be exempt from all future births and is supposed to secure absorption in the supreme essence of God. It is on account of this high nature of worship that the main hall of the Shiva temple in this town is termed the *chit-sabha* – the hall in which the true devotee acquires illimitable and supernatural powers which could be obtained only by concentrated devotion to God and which, when once acquired, could be exercised at will. Including the *chit-sabha* – the hall of supreme vision and wisdom, there are five chief halls in the Chidambaram shrine, which are called the *kanaka-sabha* – the golden hall; the *deva-sabha* – the divine hall; and the *nritta-sabha* – the hall of dancing. The special deity worshipped in the temple is called *Natesa* – the king of dancers; *Sabhesa* – the lord of the several sacred halls; and *Sabhapati* – the president of these sacred halls. The prominent idea underlying the *Sthala Purana* of Chidambaram is that the great God having perceived his own self in Himself is illuminated with wisdom and dances with very joy on account thereof; and that the devotee who visits the temple and witnesses this dance becomes himself absorbed in God. The Chidambaram shrine has thus from time immemorial been a visible symbol of a philosophic phase of the Hindu religion. It is the place where, according to Hindu beliefs, persons even of the lowest caste have attained oneness with God by sincere devotion and faith. Nanda – a pariah saint – attained eternal felicity by his devotions at Chidambram. The most orthodox of the orthodox Brahmans will never taint the reputation of this greatest of Shiva saints, who after all was only a pariah by birth. It is the only place in the whole of India where no attempt has been made to import conventional ideas of godhead into the purely philosophic basis of the Hindu religion. In keeping with this fame, Chidambram is now the seat of several Sudra monasteries, where several hundreds of Sudra mendicants are taught sanskrit. A Brahman visitor to this sacred town will be surprised to see the number of Sudras repeating the *Upanishads* in the early morning in these monasteries. To add to his wonder he will find that they have not only got by heart these sacred writings but that they understand their meaning and possess a perfect knowledge of the subject – matter which is a rare thing even with Brahmans.

Such is the merit of Chidambram. Special meritoriousness is attached by the Saivites to the Ardra festival which takes place in the month of Margasira, corresponding to the latter half of December and the first half of Janaury. As the Hindu deity Rama is supposed to have been born on a *Navami* day and Krishna on an *Ashtami* day, so Shiva in his incarnation of Natesa is considerd by the Saivites to have been born on the fullmoon day of the month of Margasira and in the constellation of Ardra-the sixth lunar mansion. On the night

7

previous to the feast the bathing of the image of the god Natesa takes place on a grand scale. Of the Hindu trinity Shiva is supposed to be fond of baths and Vishnu of ornaments. The Shiva of Chidambaram-Lord Natesa – is bathed only six times in a year, and the bath on the night previous to the Ardra feast is conducted on the grandest scale. Pilgrims and devotees flock to the hall where this bathing is performed. Pots full of milk, honey, lemon-juice, pomegranate juice, coconut water, ghee, oil, sandal paste, curds, holyashes, and other liquids and solids, considered as sacred offerings to the deity, pour in from all parts to be used on the occasion. This ceremony commences at about midnight and lasts till late in the morning. When the bathing is over the image is tastefullydecorated; and the Brahman priests of Chidambaram are considered to be adept at showing off the image to its best advantage. The decoration is done behind screens amid the hymns of praise chanted by the thousands of pilgrims and devotees who have assembled there to worship God. The choicest temple jewels in southern India, made of the finest of precious stones, are to be seen only in two shrines – Srirangam and Chidambaram. Natesa on the Ardra festival day is most superbly decorated and at about evening time is taken round on a grand procession. The most impressive scene of the Ardra festival the Anandatandavam – the dance in ecstatic joy – takes place on this occasion. The bearers of the image have a mode of marching slowly, so as to give the image the appearance of dancing. The most holy of holies – the *Garbhagriha* of the temple – is reached after a slow march of three or four hours;

and this completes the Ardra feast.

There is a queer story in connection with this feast which obtains credence with the mass of the worshippers, but which is not to be found in any of the Hindu Puranas. It is that the god Shiva left his inner apartments one night and returned home early next morning. The goddess Parvati grew jealous on this account and denied him admission. Hot words were exchanged and soon after reconciliation followed. In keeping with this legend the temple doors are shut just as the god enters at the close of the procession on the Ardra day, and questions and replies take place between two priests who represent the god and goddess. After the supposed reconciliation the doors are opened. This, as has been said already, is entirely a popular belief, having no puranic foundation.

The places in Southern India most sacred to this feast are Chidambaram in the South Arcot District, Tiruvalur in the Tanjore District, Tiruchirapalli District, and Perur in the Coimbatore District. The great Saiva philosopher – Manikkavasakar – passed his latter days in Chidambaram and worshipped Natesa. A small festival in honour of the memory of this philosopher takes place on this occasion in the temple.

# Bihu

Bihu is undoubtedly the most important festival of Assam and the Assamese. Bihu and agriculture are closely connected and it is basically a harvest festival. It is probably the biggest secular festival in India. The origin of the word 'Bihu' may be traced to the Sanskrit word Bishuban or Bishan in English may be interpreted as the equinoctical circle (equinox). Bihu is associated with the seasonal cycle. In Assam Bihu is celebrated in three parts. Each part is connected with an aspect of cultivation. It is also associated with the movement of the sun.

Bohag Bihu is the most important of the three. It is also called Rongali Bihu as it ushers in fun, laughter, song and dance. This festival coincides with Mahabishub Sankranti. It starts in the middle of April, that is on the first of Baisakh, the Assamese New Year. The winter fog disappears and the advent of spring ushers in a feeling of joy and celebration among the people, Symbolic of the exuberance which finds expression in nature. The festival starts on the last day of the year on Chaitra

Sankranti. This day is dedicated to the cow and is known as Goru Bihu or Gowali Bihu. In ancient society, a man's wealth was measured in terms of the number of cows he possessed. This led to the desire to increase the number of cattle one possessed. This finds expression in the Bihu songs. On this day, the family massage the horns of the cows with mustard oil. The forehead and horns are smeared with turmeric and kolai. Then the cowherds using special sticks take the cows for a bath. The head of each stick is split into three and stuck with bits of cucumber, pumpkin and white gourd. The cows are left free to graze. All the cowherds return home after their bath and fix the special sticks on the thatched roofs of the huts. Other members of the family take their bath after smearing themselves with turmeric and kolai. Youngsters touch the feet of the elders and have puffed rice and curd. In the evening, when the cows return home, their hooves are washed. Vermillion or sandal paste is smeared on their horns and forehead. New ropes are bought for the cows and hulls and ploughs are scoured clean. The entire North Eastern Region observes Rongali Bihu on Chaitra Sankranti with Goru or Gowali Bihu. One must go to the villages of Assam to really enjoy the rituals and songs of Gowali Bihu.

Rongali or Bohag Bihu starts on the first day of the New Year. It is colloquially known as 'Manush' Bihu. The youngsters bathe early in the morning and touch the feet of the elders. They get 'Bihuban' or gifts. Usually, a 'towel' with a red border, woven by the mother or the elder sister is given and cherished. People go visiting one another. The wandering minstrels or 'Puchuri' travel all over the villages singing Bihu songs. They are accompanied on the drums, cymbals and 'Toka' made of bamboo. Elders play with 'cowrie'. Youngsters have egg-fights and the ones who break the eggs win and the ones whose eggs are broken lose.

The most alluring part of the celebration is the collection of young men and women in some secluded area, away from the crowds. They dance. The sweet songs of Bihu echo the mood of love. Young maidens wear new 'Mehla' and the songs are about the union of hearts. The young men invite the damsels to be their brides and they readily accept. It is a day of mixed dances., betrothals and love. Girls vie with one another to weave colourful scarves for their lovers. Young men look for the loveliest Kopow orchids to present to their sweethearts. Love is the predominant theme of the dances and songs.

The third day of Rongali Bihu is also known as 'Brahmani Bihu'. The head of the family takes a bath and goes to an astrologer. The astrologer writes the family fortunes on a Nageshwar leaf. The astrologer never predicts anything bad. The householder then folds the leaf and sticks it in the thatched roof of his house. According to the ancient belief, the family will have good luck, peace and prosperity.

Songs and dances usher in the New Year to the village community. At such a time if a stranger appears in any Assamese village, he will be welcomed by one and all. This Assamese hospitality has not diminished with the economic pressures. This festival continues for seven days. It is then time to bid farewell to Bihu. This is called Bihu Dhoa'or Bihu Urua. It is a ritual held away from the village, in some forest or secluded place. Here, the villagers leave behind some implements used in the Bihu festival like drum, Toka and so on. They go back to the village. Thus ends Rongali or Bohag Bihu.

Kati Bihu or Kangali Bihu is observed on Jalabishub Sankranti in the month of Kartik. At this time the granaries are nearly empty. There is no rejoicing in this Bihu. It is devoid of pomp and grandeur. Kati Bihu is an occasion for devotion and solemnity. The whole idea behind Kati Bihu is the general expectation of a good harvest. Many prayers and rituals are held to keep away insects, birds and rodents that destroy crops. Children plant a 'tulsi' tree in their own courtyard on the last day of Aswin. For the whole month they light 'chaki-salita' (small earthen lamp lit with mustard oil) in the evening near the tulsi tree. On the Bihu day, every family lights a chaki-salita in the barn and paddy field.

Nature responds to the wishes of the people. Once more the fields become golden with corn. Magh Bihu or Bhogali Bihu coincides with Uttarayan Sankranti. It falls in the month of January-February. In winter the harvest is over and the grain is cut and stored in the granary. It is time for fulfilment. The day before Magh Bihu is known as Urhua. There is an air of happiness everywhere. Women get busy making snacks. Young men go to an open space, preferably on the bank of a river, and here they build a temporary 'Khelaghar' (for picnic). At four corners they tie the Mejhi (Bamboo sticks) in a temple like structure. When the work is over they hold a midnight feast with songs and dances. As the day dawns it ushers in the month of Magh. Then, one young man takes a dip in the river and sets fire to the Mehjhis. A few articles are also thrown into the fire. When the Mehjhis are burnt the villagers bathe in the river. On their way home, they pick up bits and piece of the burnt Mejhis and throw them in their orchards. It is an ancient belief that the fruits will be sweeter. The women treat the menfolk and children to snacks. On this day, many games are held. Bull-fight, although very popular at one time, are dying out now. In the days of the Rajas, sword-fights and falcon-races were held.

It is clear that Bihu is derived from the fertility cult. A lot of research has been done on the origin of Bihu. According to some experts, it was prevalent in some form in South-Eastern China, which again was closely connected with North-Eastern India. The people of Assam adjusted the Mongolian festival to their taste and culture. It can be said with certainty that the Bihu festival did not come from the Aryans.

This festival was mainly started by the Kom tribe. The 'Mini' tribe celebrates two other bihus, apart from the usual three. One is 'Ahu', that is, before the planting of the Aus paddy and the other after cutting the 'Amon' paddy. The Garo festival is closely linked to the sowing and cutting of the paddy. The Adivasis of Arunachal Pradesh, like their counterparts in the plains, celebrate the harvesting of fruits.

Salung, a festival which spreads over seven days is held in the month of January-February. The women of the Adi tribe, like their sisters from the plains clean their pots, pans and houses. They prepare eats beforehand. The men leave their homes and go hunting in the jungle for ten days. Whatever they hunt is divided equally among the villagers. The Adi bachelors set up a huge fire in their own homes. They sit around the fire and spend the night in an orgy of drinking and merrymaking. Perhaps Magh Bihu originated from one such primitive festival.

Honouring the cattle and writing the future on the Nageshwar leaf might have come much later. The Buddhists of Assam take out the image of Buddha from the temple on Bihu day. Whilst bathing the image, they sprinkle each other with water. Some take their religious vows.

During the British Raj, a few so called westernised Indians like Dhakial Phukon, Ratneswar Mohonto, Gunaiviram Barua and so on, tried to stop the Bihu songs and dances as they believed that they were detrimental to culture. However Bihu continues to be a popular festival with the Assamese even today.

# The Vinayaka Chaturthi

Vinayak Chaturthi is set apart for the sole worship of Ganesh, the common deity of all Hindus. As he is supposed to be very fond of rice puddings, these dishes are cooked on a very large scale in every Hindu house and offered to the god, to be consumed by the members of the family, after the worship is over. A fresh image of Ganesh in clay is made and worshipped on this day. One hundred and eight different names of this god are repeated after the preliminary ceremonies and 108 different flowers are thrown in worship over him. The origin of this worship is prehistoric. Yudhisthira, the hero of the *Mahabharata,* Damayanti, the queen of the Nishada King Nala, Indra, the Lord of the Heavens and even Krishna, the expounder of the *Bhagavatgita* are said to have devoutly worshipped Ganesh and to have obtained their desired ends. Vinayaka or Ganesh is the eldest son of Shiva and Parvati, or of Parvati only, according to the following legend, as he sprang from the dirt of her body. Shiva had gone from home and Parvati was left alone on the Kailasa; she wished to have a bath and not liking the idea of any person entering the house then, she rubbed her body with her hands and from the dirt that rolled off produced a figure to which she gave life and named Ganesh. She then asked Ganesh to sit at the door and allow no one, whoever he might be, to come in till she had finished her bath. Ganesh sat at his duty and while Parvati was bathing inside, Shiva returned home. He wanted to enter his house, but Ganesh would not allow him. After trying in vain to persuade him with gentle words, the great god used threats which, however, had no effect. He was at last, compelled to cut off Ganesh's head and force his way in. When the goddess who was within perceived her lord entering and when she came to know that Ganesh had been murdered, she would not speak to Shiva until her attendant was restored to life. In order to do this, Shiva gave orders to his army of the Bhutaganas to find the first living creature that slept with its head turned towards the north, to cut off its head and to fit it into Ganesh's body. The Bhutas searched and searched for a very long time and at last found an elephant asleep with its head to the north, and cutting off its head, they brought it and fixed it to Ganesh's body, and lo! he rose up Ma man in body and elephant in face. This story also accounts for the belief of Hindus to avoid the northern aspect in sleep.

Vinayaka is the eldest son of Shiva and Parvati and one of the most popular deities of India. He is the male Minerva and the Janus of public ways. His shrine is in every Hindu village.

He is worshipped in every Hindu house. Every school boy begins his lessons after offering his usual prayers to Vinayaka. Every merchant commences his operation after first propitiating this deity. In marriages and every other kind of religious ceremony, Vinayaka is the first god whose help is invoked. Almost all the standard works in Sanskrit and the Vernacular languages begin with an invocation of the help of Ganesh. Vinayaka's figure is represented as elephant in face and man in body. The elephant's head is regarded as the emblem of sagacity. In his image he is always seated at his ease, with his legs folded under him on a lotus throne. He has four arms and they hold an elephant's trunk, a noose, a mace, and a *Modaka* (rice pudding). He wears a crown. His ears are adorned with jewels and his forehead *vibhuti*—the sacred ashes. He wears a garland of pearls and precious stones round his neck. He is worshipped under the different names of Vinayaka, Ganesh, Ganapati, Pillaiyar, etc. As this most popular deity is worshipped in almost every village, there is a belief among certain people that he is the god of the Sudras and lower orders, who are generally uneducated. As an authority for this belief, the following couplet is sometimes quoted:-

Viparanam daivatam Sambhuh

Kshatriyanam tu Madhavah

Vaisyanam tu bhaved Brahma

Sudranam Gananayakah!!

19

The above verse means that Shiva is the god of the Brahmans, Vishnu of the Kshatrivas, Brahma of the vaisyas, and Ganesh of the Sudras. This is a most fanciful verse, which is not at all corroborated by any other authority. If any regard is to be paid to this couplet, then no Brahman can worship Vishnu and no Vaisya can worship Shiva, facts which are absurd on their very face, as testified by both the ancient and modern ways of Hindu faith.

Ganesh worship is a prehistoric one and it goes without saying that the couplet sometimes quoted as an authority that Ganesh is the god of the Sudras is unfounded. On the other hand, he is worshipped by the highest class of Brahmans. There are also special sects who are called Ganapatiyas, whose sole devotion is to this deity. Vinayaka is the deity that rules over good and bad alike-controlling the evil in every case and preventing hindrances to success. He controlled all those qualities which overcame hindrances in every undertaking with their usual accompaniments-good living, plenty, prosperity, and peace. This is the one great and real reason for the popularity of the worship of this deity.

There is always a small shrine of Vigneswara, attached to all Shiva temples. In the Vishnu temples too he is worshipped as *Tumbikkaialvar* – the sage of the elephant's trunk – and as *Vishvaksena*. Sometimes he has his own temples too. As he is the favourite son of Shiva, he receives honours equal to Shiva. His image is with sincere devotion adored by men and women alike. He is supposed to represent the several personifications of sagacity, shrewdness, patience, and learning. As a test of his wisdom, it is related that when he was a child and playing in company with his brother Subrahmanya, Shiva promised to present a mango to him who made a circuit round the world and returned first. Subrhamanya summoned his peacock, mounted it and was ready for the journey. But Ganesh calmly went round Shiva, his father, and demanded the fruit. "But you never went round the world,"said Shiva. "What is the world, but your own holy self? I went round you. *Ergo,* I went round the world," was Ganesh's wise reply. Shiva was of course convinced, praised Ganesh for his shrewdness, and gave him the promised fruit, which however, he shared with Subrahmanya. The peculiarity of this deity is that his worship is combined as it were with that of every other god. All sects unite in claiming him as their own. It is for this reason that his shrines are found generally associated with those of other deities – Shiva and Vishnu. The largest temple built solely in honour of Ganesh in India is the Uchchippillaiyar temple on the top of the famous and beautiful rock at Tiruchirapalli.

Though this god is invoked on several occasions during the year, there is a special day in every year which is set apart particularly for his worship, and this day is called the *Vinayaka Chaturthi* day, which falls on the fourth lunar day of the bright half of the month of Simha. The Tamils term this day *Pillaiyar Chavutti* day.

Of all the figures in Hindu Mythology, that of Ganesh or Pilaiyar must be most familiar to every European. In the

21

bathing ghat of every river and underneath the pipal tree will be seen a figure in a sitting posture, short and stout, with a protuberant stomach and four hands, riding a mouse and with the body of man and the head of an elephant. This is the image of Ganesh or Pillaiyar, and there is not a single village in the whole of India which does not possess at least half a dozen of these familiar images. The elephant head has only one full tusk and the other appears cut off in the middle, the result of a scuffle between Ganesh and Parasurama. The "bellygod" is on this account called *Ekadanta,* or the single-tusked. Ganesh is said to have written the *Mahabharata* at the dictation of Vyasa – for it is said that the latter was so quick in repeating the epic that no mortal could have managed to follow him.

# Diwali Or Deepavali

The festival of lights is celebrated in the month of Kartik (October-November) on Krishna Chaturdashi. The moon rotates around the earth in 28 days. We have fourteen days of light and fourteen days of darkness. Krishna Chaturdashi is the darkest night of the dark period. Diwali is one of the three festivals celebrated all over India along with Holi and Dussera. This festival is different in form and nature from all other festivals. It is associated with the cult of Kali.

The mythological background of this festival is many and varied. It is said that when Rama returned to Ayodhya after defeating Ravana in Lanka, the people of Ayodhya celebrated the event with lights and fireworks on Krishna Chaturdashi.

In the month of Kartik, Narakasura, a demon, took into captivity all the gopinis (shepherdesses) of Brindavan and Mathura. Krishna was furious and in his anger he killed Narakasura. All the gopinis were rescued. The event was celebrated with lights and fireworks all over Mathura and Brindavan.

Yet again the story goes that the Gods wanted the 'Amrit Kumbha' so as to get the elixir of life and conquer death. They joined the demons in this venture. Mainak mountain was used as the churning rod and Basuki, the snake was twisted round the mountain to be used as the churning rope. The God and the demons then began to churn the ocean in unison. The poison from Basuki vitiated the water and the demons became unconscious. It was then that the Amrit Kumbha arose from the water. The Gods drank and became immortal. This memorable event was celebrated with lights and fireworks by the Gods.

On the histrical front we have Chandragupta II who took the name of Sakari Vikramaditya after conquering the Sakas. He returned to his capital Magadh in triumph. His subjects celebrated his great victory with lights and fireworks.

The sociological aspect of this festival is very interesting. We find evidences of the worship of Kali by the non-Aryan tribes-Katya, Kaushiki, Parnasabari and so on. The goddess

Kali was worshipped on the darkest night of the month, i.e. on Krishna Chaturdashi to ward off death. She was perceived as someone fearful and naked. Darkness was her only apparel. Due to the darkness, the worship of Kali took place amidst illuminations. Crackers were burst to ward off evil spirits. With the passage of time, this festival entered into the Aryan cult of worship. Gradually the fearful appearance was replaced by different forms. Kali assumed different names in different regions. In Andhra Pradesh and in Karnataka she is Chamundeshwari, in Kanchi we have Kamakshi, Meenakshi in Madurai and further down South, she is Mukh Ambika. In the eastern region she came to be known as Mahakali.

Kali Puja was abandoned in the east, specially in Bengal. In the 16th century, Krishnananda Arambagish of Nadia (a learned pundit) reintroduced Kali puja in its earliest form. Gradually Kali puja was joined to the worship of Shiva. The original dead body (as Kali was the goddess of death) turned into Shiva. It is a pecular feature of Bengal and an interesting Bengali trait that no matter whatever fearful cult is introduced, the Bengalis turn it into a popular household phenomenon. Characteristically the fearful Kali has become Shyama, Bhadrokali, Rakshakali, Siddhakali and so on. Kali puja in its most popular form is the worship of Kali and Shiva, the most popular God. This festival is now an Indian festival and Diwali or Deepavali is a festival of lights and fireworks.

# Durga Puja

**S**miling blue skies trimmed with fleecy white clouds, gentle breeze, warm sunshine and the 'kash' flowers usher in the month of Aswin (September-October). It is time for Durga Puja, the main festival of Bengal, bringing with it new hope to the hearts of all Bengalis. Durga Puja or Durgotsava starts off a chain of festivals which end

with Saraswati Puja. Mahalaya and the pre-dawn recitation from the Chandi announce the advent of Durgotsava. Preparations and expectations culminate in the Puja days, Shashti, Saptami, Ashtami and Nabami. The beat of drums, the clash of cymbals, the ringing of bells, dances before the image of Durga, incense wafting in the air, all form an integral part of Durga Puja. All too soon it is Bijoyam the day when the images are taken in a procession and immersed in the river. Bengalis go back to their mundane lives to wait another year to welcome the goddess.

Durga Puja, as we know it today, is a festival that binds together people from all walks of life, irrespective of caste, creed and religion. It is a community festival, though in some houses they still have private pujas. Durgotsava has turned out to be a source of livelihood for people in different spheres. The image-maker, the priest, the florists, the dhaki (drum-beater), grocers, confectioners and volunteers are all part and parcel of this festival. It is a time to exchange gifts. This is a season for new clothes. The puja generates enthusiasm as well as income for countless people.

A notable feature of Durga Puja is the Puja Issue of a magazine. This cultural aspect is a literary offering on the eve of Mahalaya. This unique feature of Bengal reminds us that it has always been in the forefront of culture. Associated with the Puja, cultural functions and melas (fairs) are held. These melas create mass contact and develop various folk arts and cottage industries.

A peep into the past presents us with a rich background of the mythological and historical aspects of this great festival. Durga was a Puranic Goddess. In the Puranas, the struggle between the Gods and demons or 'asuras' is mentioned. The Gods could not subdue Mahisasura, the king of demons, who drove the gods out of heaven. They went to Vishnu who told them that it would be possible for someone other than a God to defeat Mahisasura. The name Tilottoma and not Durga is found in the Puranas. She was created with all the special attributes. Shiva gave her his trident, Vishnu his die, the spear was given by Yama, Agni gave a dart, Kubera a club, Kala a sword, Surya a quiver full or arrows for a magical bow given by Vayu; Varuna provided her with a conch to announce her victory; Viswakarma a battle axe and Indra his thunderbolt. Himavan gave her a mount – a ferocious lion. She was also adorned with jewels.

She subjugated Mahisasura and is also known as Mahisasurmardini, who disappeared into nothingness. Mahisasura is identified with a black buffalo.

The war between the asuras and the Gods took place in spring, the season for war. It is said that Ram invoked the blessings of Chandi in Autumn before attacking Lanka. This was not the proper time for war. Therefore Rama had to invoke Chandi so as to be victorious. The Chandi-worship of Rama was called "Akal Bodhan" the untimely worship.

Another myth centers around Parvati, the daughter of Menaka and Himalaya. She unwillingly married Shiva. The Durga mythology slowly crept into the social mainstream and gave rise to poignant yet common social feelings. Durga has other common houselold names like Uma, Gouri, Lalita and so on.

The very name Durga is not Aryan but Asianic. This name

Durga, came from aboriginal sources like the Santhal folk lore. The kingdom of Champa (modern Pataliputra, Magadh) was ruled by Harmaid Durga. The Aryans could not defeat him. They engaged a beautiful courtesan to entice Harmaid Durga. She was so successful that, when the Aryans attacked, Harmaid Durga, busy with his courtesan did not bother to protect his kingdom. Consequently Harmaid Durga was killed and the Aryans worshipped the courtesan. The feminine of Durga should rightfully be Durgi. The worship of Durga became the annual Aryan festival and the Durga cult was established among the Aryans. Incidentally, the Aryans called the non-Aryans 'dashyu', 'dashya', 'dasa' (slave) and subdued them. This explains the presence of the black buffalo.

Durga Puja was not prevalent anywhere in Bengal before the 15th century. In the folk songs of the Bauls (wandering minstrels of North and West Bengal, the arrival of Gouri in Autumn, has been sung.

The historical evidence of Durga Puja can be traced to the time of Hossain Shah Sultan of Bengal. It was the Golden Age of Bengal, the end of the fifteenth century. Political power was in the hands of the zamindars. The zamindars of North Bengal were all powerful. There was great rivalry between the zamindars of Dinajpur and Malda for social supremacy. The zamindars of Dinajpur initiated Durga Puja. Akal Bodhan, on the day when Rama worshipped Durga. He spent 9,00,000. There was great pomp and pageantry and the climate was excellent as it was autumn.

The zamindar of Malda to out-beat his rival performed Basanti Puja according to Puranic tradition in Chaitra and spent 9,50,000. From the next year, both did Durga Puja in Autumn.

Later, the centre of Muslim rule shifted from Gaur to Dhaka. The zamindars flourshed in East Bengal. They vied with each other and Durga Puja was performed by most. In the eighteenth century, it spread to other parts of Bengal. It is difficult to pinpoint the date but Radhakanto Deb and Kalikrishna Thakur brought the festival to Calcutta.

The Maratha dacoits or Borgis would annually invade Bengal. They adopted Durga Puja and carried it westward with them. It is performed with different names in many parts of the country, particulary in the Eastern region and specially in Bengal. In Nepal it is performed as Chandi Puja.

Durga Puja as we know it today has undergone a vast change from the past. It is performed by Bengalis all over the world. Twelve friends or Baro Yar first joined together and performed a community Durga Puja. It came to be known as Baroyari, then Baroari.

A few Durga Pujas in Calcutta are organized wholly by women, Durgotsav is now a community festival and has spread to every nook and cranny of Bengal.

# The Hindus and the Eclipse

The Hindus were the first to have correct and scientific ideas about eclipses. Varahamihira, the greatest Hindu astronomer who flourished in the sixth century A.D., has described the phenomena of eclipses in the same way as any astronomer of the twentieth century would do. But with most Hindus the eclipse is the swallowing of the sun and the moon for a time by a demon called Rahu. Rahu is also one of the nine planets in the astronomy of the Hindus, the ascending node. If any Hindu calendar is consulted for the figure of an eclipse, Rahu, in the form of a monstrous serpent or dragon, will be seen to grasp the sun. Thus the common Hindu believes the eclipse to be a great calamity that has come over the luminaries. He has to fast for six hours before the commencement of the eclipse. During the course of the eclipse he has to perform certain ceremonies. As soon as the first contact takes place he bathes and offers prayers to the Manes. After the last phase of the eclipse he bathes again, offers certain prayers and returns home. During the course of the eclipse he stays by the side of a river or on the sea-shore. River-baths and sea-baths are performed on this occasion to propitiate the *Manes*. Some devout Hindus go on a pilgrimage to Rameswaram or Benares to plunge themselves in the waters of the ocean or the Ganges during the eclipse.

The eclipse must take must take place on some asterism or other, and if that asterism happens to be that in which any Hindu was born, he has to perform some special ceremonies to absolve himself from impending evil. Every Hindu who was born in the asterism in which the eclipse takes place considers it as a foreboding of some calamity for him in that year. He makes a plate of gold or silver or of palm-leaf, according to his means, and ties it on his forehead, with Sanskrit verses inscribed over it. He sits with this plate for some time, performs certain ceremonies, bathes with the plate untied and presents it to a Brahman with some fee, ranging from four annas to several thousands of rupees, according to his means. Maharajas give large donations to Brahmans on this occasion. Nearly 90 per cent. of the copper-plate grants of the Vijaynagar period of the 15th and 16th centuries A.D. are donations of villages and of property to Brahamans by the Hindu kings of Vijaynagar on the occasion of either a solar or a lunar eclipse. Even now in Cochin, Mysore, Baroda and other areas, the Brahmans are most munificently remunerated on the occasion of an eclipse.

The belief that an eclipse is a calamity to the sun or the

moon is such a strong Hindu belief that no marriages take place in the months in which an eclipse falls. Even the most educated Hindu who has taken his degree, with special distinction in astronomy probably, undergoes all the Hindu rites on the occasion. The eclipse time is considered a most auspicious time for mastering incantations for exorcising the evil effects of serpent bite, or scorpion-sting, and of devils, and many specialists in these directions may be seen standing in water and muttering these incantations.

# Ganeshutsav

The worship of Ganesh is prevalent all over India. Ganesh is generally worshipped before any religious festival. Ganesh Chaturthi falls on the fourth day of the bright half of the month of Bhadon or Bhadrapad (August-September).

Social background:- No other festival portrays so vividly the social evolution as the gradual evolution of Ganesh. The worship of Ganesh can be traced to the pre-Aryan age. In the northern regions Ganesh was a tribal God of the different Koms. Their totem was the elephant. The mouse that is seen with Ganesh was also a totem of a lesser tribe. Shiva

was also a pre-Aryan God, as is obvious from the seals of the Mohenjodaro and Harappa culture. Democracy was the norm among the ancient tribes.

Gana means tribe or adivasi. Gana-isha means leader of the people. When the Aryans appeared on the scene, Ganesh was known as "Vignaraj" or leader of obstruction. The small tribal democracies were a challenge to the Aryan power-kingship and Brahmanism. It was the Mauryas who overcame the tribes and their destruction was advocated by none other than Chanyaka in Kautilya's `Arthashashtra'. With the defeat of the hill tribes, the Ganesh cult which was already prevalent, was adopted by the Aryans to placate the people. Conflict and assimilation led to Ganesh becoming an Aryan God from a tribal one. Ganesh now became Sidhi Raj, symbol of success or Sidhidata Ganesh. From a tribal or local God, Ganesh was elevated to the higher echleons by the reference to his elephant's trunk as that of Indra's pet elephant, Airabat. There were fifty different forms of Ganesh within the different tribes. Ganesh is known by various names like Ekdanta, Kapil, Lamboder, Sumukh, Vighnashan, Ganadhyaksha and so on.

The word 'siddhi' literally means 'letter'. Ganesh's role in spreading writing was acknowledged long ago. In this context, the writing of the Mahabharata is important. Vyasdev could not write. He wanted someone to take down his dictation. Finally, Ganesh agreed to write on the condition that Vyasdev did not stop dictating. As this was an impossible proposition, Vyasdev also made a counter condition. Ganesh had to understand what he wrote. He used such difficult lines or 'slokas' that Ganesh had to stop and ponder. This gave Vyasdev time to think of his next lines. In short, Ganesh was accepted by the Aryans as the propagator of learning. The worship of Ganesh at the start of any festival was established.

Mythological background:- The mythological background of Ganesh was developed much later in the Middle Ages. There are various interesting stories of the birth of Ganesh in the Matsya Purana, Varaha Purana, Shiva Purana and Brahmavaivarta Purana.

Matsya Purana is the source of the most popular story. In this story, the birth of Ganesh is attributed solely to Parvati. Once while bathing, Parvati created a man from the oil, ointments and impurities of her body. Parvati sprinkled Ganges water and breathed new life into him. She asked him to guard her from intruders. When Shiva appeared, Ganesh refused him entry. This infuriated Shiva and he cut off Ganesh's head. In order to calm Parvati who grieved over her Ganesh, Shiva ordered the head of whatever was seen first to be brought to him. It so happened, that an elephant's head was found and Shiva fitted it to the body of Ganesh. Parvati was not too pleased with the appearance of Ganesh. She was promised that Ganesh would be the leader of the Vinayakas (minor deities). Ganesh is therefore also known as Vinayaka. He was to be worshipped at the beginning of all religious rituals, to remove obstacles. Vignabarta is another name for Ganesh. Eventually Parvati was pacified.

According to another legend, Parvati asked for Vishnu's help as she had no child. Vishnu, in deference to her wishes and pleased with her devotion, decided to be born as her son. Parvati invited all the Gods and Godesses to a feast on the birth of her son. All saw and blessed the baby except Sani (saturn). Sani explained that his wife had put a curse on him. Anything he saw which gave him pleasure would break into pieces. Parvati proudly declared that her baby was Vishnu himself and he would ward off all evils. Thus assured, Sani came forward to look at the beautiful baby. At once the baby's head flew off. The Gods rushed here and there as the bereaved Parvati wailed. One god saw an elephant and brought the head to Parvati. As the head was fixed to the body, the baby again came to life. Parvati was not pleased with the appearance of her son. Shiva then promised to make him leader of the Ganas (people). The child was named Ganesh from Gana-isha (leader of the people).

Yet another story tells us how once the Gods went to Kailash, in the Himalayas to meet Shiva. Brahma rode on a swan, Vishnu on an eagle and Ganapati on his rat. When climbing up the mountain slope, Ganapati slipped and fell. Only the Moon or Chandra saw the incident and smiled at the spectacle of Ganapati rolling down the mountain slope. The enraged Ganapati cursed Chandra and said that whoever looked at Chandra would be accused of a crime and be looked down upon. Chandra, escorted by the other Gods, went to Ganapati and begged for mercy. At last Ganapati relented and agreed to take back his curse on one condition. The curse would remain effective for one day in the year-Ganesh Chaturthi. If anyone looks at the moon, then the best way to ward off the curse is to indulge in a small crime and thus besaved from being charged with a serious crime.

According to the Scriptures, not only mortals but also the Gods worshipped Ganesh on different occasions. Brahma prayed to him before starting creation, Shiva before conquering the demon Tripura, Durga before destroying Mahisasura, Kamadeva before conquering the Universe, Vishnu worshipped Ganesh before defeating Bali the demon king and finally, Seshanaga, before carrying the earth on his head.

In the east, particularly in Bengal, Ganesh is worshipped, white ushering in new crops, new accountancy with the New Year. It is primarily a people's festival all over Bengal.

Ganesh Utsav has a totally new connotation in Maharashtra. It is the major festival of the state and starts on Ganesh Chaturthi. Here he is Siddi Vinayak, symbol of Hindu Kshatriya strength and power. The credit for establishing Ganesh Utsav as a national festival goes to Bal Gangadhar Tilak. Greek history taught him that the independent city states of Greece came together through the Olympic Games. Tilak established Ganesh Utsav as a social festival. The aim of doing so was to unite the people in their struggle against British imperialism. Bal Gangadhar Tilak established Ganapati Utsav in Maharashtra in 1892 as a festival of the common people.

Ganesh Chaturthi falls at the tail end of the monsoon. Ten

days of festivities transform the life of the people into one of fun and laughter. Idols of Ganesh are installed in most houses. Community worship too is prevalent. The images come in a variety of colours, sizes and prices. Some are so large that they have to be set up at the time of installation. The images are carried in processions amidst the chanting of prayers. Homes are beautifully decorated. The streets look like fairyland. The images are installed on artistically decorated rostrums accompanied by religious rites. Public functions like plays, musical extravanganzas and so on are arranged. A devotee must keep a vigil through the night, near the image of Ganesh. The god is said to be fond of sweets like laddoos. People offer this 'prasad' to the lord. Many devotees pay for the prasad on a particular day of the festival at community pujas. People and groups vie with one another to to make Ganesh Utsav as grand as possible. The whole of Maharashtra pours out on to the streets to see the images and the illuminations in the evenings. The tenth day is the day of immersion. All the images are lined up to be paraded through the city in the evening. The images of Ganesh are carried on all kinds of transport to the accompaniment of music. Cries of "Ganapati Bappa Moriya" rend the air, invoking the lord's blessings and wishing for his return the next year. Priests chant prayers and people dance and sing and sprinkle 'gulal' on each other. The images are immersed in the river, lakes and ponds. A pall of gloom and uneasy calm spreads over the entire state as people bid farewell to their lord. They wait anxiously and hopefully for his return the next year.

# *Holi*

Holi is the most popular of the three Indian festivals – Holi, Diwali and Dussehra. It is also the most secular festival although it has a touch of religiosity. This festival is celebrated on the Full Moon Day in the month of Phalgun (February-March).

Holi is the oldest festival and has taken different forms since the pre-historic times. It was a festival adopted by both Aryans and Non-Aryans alike. This festival is symbolic of new crops and the new year. It is a farewell to the past and an invocation to everything new.

This festival is known by different names in different parts of the country. 'Phalguni Purnima' has its source in the phagua or phag, the powder used in Holi. The original colours used were red and green. Red as a symbol of desire and green stands for youth and vigour. In Bengal it is known as 'Dol Purnima' from the swing on which sat Radha and Krishna. Orissa celebrates 'Dol Jatra'. In Western India, inGoa and in the Konkan, it is called 'Simagh' in celebration of youth and vitality. It is 'Madan Daman' or 'Kamayan' in South India. Kamayan represents the fulfilment of desire. North India has just 'Holi' or'Hori'.

Holi has three distinct aspects. It is symbolic of hope for new crops, youth and vigour as well as an invocation to the new year. It is said Phalgun was the last month of the year as stated in the Bavishya Purana. Some scholars are of the opinion that as the year comes back as 'dol' the festival was called 'Dol Purnima'. This festival heralds the advent of spring. People are in a jubilant mood and feel rejuvenated.

The usual legends surround this festival. Hiranyakashipu, a mighty king worshipped Shiva and was fanatically opposed to Vishnu. His son Prahlad, on the other hand, was an ardent devotee of Vishnu. The father tried to destroy his son but failed. His sister Holika was immune to fire. He employed Holika to enter the fire with Prahlad on her lap. The unexpected happened. Holika was burnt to ashes and Prahlad emerged unscathed. The worshippers of Vishnu, celebrated the occasion by burning the effigy of Holika. They celebrated the event with phag or powder on Phalguni Purnima Day. Holi was celebrated by the Vaishnavas, the followers of Vishnu.

The Vaishanav cult found expression in Radha and Krishna. The festival of Radha and Krishna on the swing or 'dola' is 'Dol Purnima'. According to Srimadbhagvata, Putana, a female demon, tried to kill Krishna, who was the eighth, incarnation of Vishnu. When Krishna was a baby, his uncle, King Kansa ordered a general massacre of all babies. Putana, in the disguise of a woman, suckled infants to death. Krishna, knowing her for what she was, sucked her lifeblood and destroyed her. In Mathura and Brindavan, where the Krishna cult flourishes, the effigy of Putana is burnt. It is here, in the birth place of Krishna, that Holi is celebrated with traditional songs, dances and the spraying of colours.

Yet another legend associated with Holi is the destruction of Kamadeva, the God of Love by Shiva. Parvati, the daughter of Menaka and Himalaya was deeply in love with Shiva. At that time, Shiva was immersed in deep meditation and took no notice of her. Kama, in order to help Parvati, disturbed Shiva's meditation. The enraged God, with the power of his third eye, reduced Kama to ashes. Later, he was restored to life at the behest of Parvati. The meditation period of Shiva is considered to be the seasonal cycle, winter. The interruption leading to his marriage with Parvati signifies new life and fulfilment.

'Dol Purnima' is also the birthday of Gouranga or Chaitanya Mahaprabhu, a sixteenth century Vaishnava saint of Bengal. 'Dol Purnima' therefore, has special significance for the followers of Vishnu.

The social customs connected with Holi are universal. The ancient Greeks and Romans, celebrated Baccalian, a fertility cult. In Europe, May Flower Day was celebrated and on this day free mixing among the youth was encouraged. According to the ancient belief, the Sky was the father and the Earth the mother and the horizon was the mating place. In Egypt, the concept was exactly the reverse. The ancient festival was celebrated by the side of the field. Holi, the most popular and yet secular festival, is celebrated by all, cutting across barriers of caste, creed and religion. People enjoy putting colour on one another. The young seek the blessing of elders. It is a time for free mixing and taboos are ignored. It is a time of hope and joy because spring is in the air.

# The Srijayanti or Krishnashtami

L ord Krishna's birthday, *Srijayanti* or *Krishnashtami*, is the most popular festival in the whole of India. These two are the names by which this festival is called by the Vaishnavas, while among the Smartas it is known as *Gokulashtami,* and in Northern India as *Janmashtami.* Whatever the name, this festive celebration of the birth of Lord Krishna is observed as a holy day by all Hindus throughout India. According to the *Puranas* Krishna was born on the 8th lunar day *(Ashtami)* of the waning moon of the month of *Sravana* at midnight, upon the moon's entrance into *Rohini asterism*. On account of this sacred occasion a fast is held on the day preceding the date of his birth, the fast being broken as usual by a feast on the following day. The observance of the fast varies with different sects. The followers of the *Smriti*-Smartas-commence their fast with the commencement of the lunation whenever that takes place; the Vaishnavas and the Madhvas regulate their fast by the moon's passage through the asterism of *Rohini*.

Krishna is the most popular deity throughout the whole of India and is considered as the eighth *Avatar* or incarnation of Vishnu, one of the Hindu Trinity, and the following is a brief account of Krishna's history as collected from the several *Puranas*.

In days gone by there reigned in Mathurna, a most wicked and unpopular king, named Kansa, who had a cousin named Devaki married to Vasudeva, of the lunar race. On the date of the latter's marriage, Kansa, the tyrant, drove the car in which Devaki and Vasudeva were conducted in procession. As the procession passed along the streets an unknown voice, deep as thunder, came from above. "Oh you fool, Kansa! The eighth child of the lady in the car that you are now driving will put an end to your atrocious life." As soon as Kansa heard this ominous voice, he became greatly enraged and attempted to put Devaki to death thereby preventing to possibility of the birth of his future enemy. But Vasudeva argued with the tyrant and pacified him by promising to deliver into his hand all the children that Devaki may bring forth. Kansa satisfied with this assurance desisted from putting his threat into execution, and true to his promise Vasudeva handed over to Kansa's custody the first six children that were born to Devaki. Balarama, the seventh child of Devaki, was saved by divine interference and Krishna was the eighth son. Of course Kansa had placed strict guard throughout the palace to prevent the eighth son from being in any way saved. How then was Krishna saved? Vasudeva, as soon as the eighth child was born, took it and went out. The guards of the palace were all charmed by *Yoganidra*- a kind of hypnotic sleep. Rain was pouring down in torrents that night, and to protect the baby from the heavy rain, Sesha, the many-headed sepent, followed Vasudeva and spread his hood over the child's head. The Jumnu was flowing full and it had to be crossed. Though the river was usually deep and dangerous with whirlpools, the waters at that time went down, running only knee deep. Thus by divine favour the several obstacles were overcome and the other side of the river was reached. There was a cowherd there named Nanda, whose wife Yashoda had delivered a female child. Vasudeva placed his son in the daughter's place, while Yashoda was also under the spell of magic sleep, and quickly returned home carrying away the female child. When Yashoda awoke she found that she had been delivered of a son and rejoiced at it.

Yashoda's female child was now placed by Vasudeva in the bed of Devaki, no suspicions being aroused in anyone's mind. The guards who were set to watch by Kansa were awakened by the cry of the new-born babe and starting up they sent word at once to their master. Kansa immediately repaired to the mansion of Vasudeva and seized hold of the infant. In vain did Devaki entreat him to spare her child; but the tyrant ruthlessly dashed it against a stone, when lo! it rose into the sky and expanded into a gigantic form and laughed aloud, striking terror into the hearts of on-lookers, and addressed Kansa in a thundering voice-"What avails with the belief that thy enemy is destroyed? *He* is born that shall kill thee, the mighty one amongst the gods." Thus saying the being vanished.

Kansa was greatly alarmed. He called a big council and ordered active search to be made for whatever young children there may be on earth and ordered that every boy in whom they observed signs of unusual vigour be put to death without any remorse. Notwithstanding all these precautions, Balarama and Krishna were growing up at the abode of Nanda, where they were roaming in the woods and joining in the sports of herdsmen's sons and daughters. When he attained to man's estate Krishna proceeded to Gujarat, built Dwarka and transferred to that place all the inhabitants of Mathura, after killing Kansa in combat.

*Krishnashtami* is the festival which is celebrated in honour of the birthday of Krishna. At about midnight, on the *Ashtami* night, a clay image of Krishna in the form of a baby is made in every Hindu house and worshipped. Several dishes of sweets are offered to the god, to be consumed afterwards by the inmates of the house. Apart from its importance from a religious point of view the feast is very popular with Hindu children on account of the sweets that are distributed to them on the occasion. A superstitious belief is current amongst the Hindus that as Krishna, who was born in the asterism of *Rohini,* was the cause of the death of his maternal uncle Kansa, the birth of a male child in that asterism forbodes evil to the maternal uncle of that child; and there were instances in old days in which such children were put to death. But this superstitious belief is fast dying out.

# The Krittika

The Krittika is a feast in honour of the glory of Shiva. The legend regarding this feast is as follows: Brahma and Vishnu had a dispute among themselves as to who was the superior of the two, and appealed to Shiva. To decide the superiority, Shiva devised a test. He said that he would stand up as an all-pervading pillar of fire, that Brahma should traverse the sky and discover the top of the pillar, and that Vishnu should find his way to the nether world and discover the foot of it. Brahma called at once his swan vehicle and started, and Vishnu assumed the form of a boar and went on boring and boring to the nether world and down to discover the foot. He who returned first and reported what he was asked to see, was to be pronounced the superior of the two. That was the test of superiority. So Brahma and Vishnu were very busy travelling one to the upper and the other to the nether world. They are said to have gone on and on for several *Yugas* (years) with no avail. While Brahma was travelling up he observed a *Ketaki* (Tamil: *Talambu*) flower, the sweet scented flower of the screwpine, travelling down towards the earth. It is stated that Brahma stopped the flower and asked him to relate his history. "O, I was on the head of Shiva several centuries ago. I left it and am going down to the earth. O, what a long journey I have had! How far is the earth yet from this place? And who are you, please, and what is your object in travelling up," asked the flower. Brahma:- "I am Brahma, and was asked by Shiva to discover the top of his head. I left the earth several *Yugas* ago. If what you say is true, I have not done half the way yet. But will you mind doing me a small favour? Vishnu and I were asked by Shiva to discover his head and foot, respectively. I shall say that I saw the head, and cite you as my witness. You must confirm this as you say that you occupied once that part of Shiva's body"

"Agreed," said the screwpine flower, for, as he had a long journey to perform to reach the earth, he liked the idea of securing a companion in Brahma for his travels and this he could gain by uttering a petty lie. So Brahma and the *Ketaki* flower started together on their downward journey and came to Shiva after several *yugas.* Brahma, of course, had carefully got by heart what he had heard from the *Ketaki* about the head of Shiva. As soon as they reached the earth, Brahma said to Shiva:-"Holy Sir! I have seen your head." Shiva realized by his superior powers that it was impossible. Still, to prove that Brahma was uttering a lie, he asked him to describe it. Brahma repeated the story that he had heard from the flower and cited the *Ketaki* as his witness. "Vile wretch," said Shiva to the screwpine, "as you have uttered a falsehood before me, may you never be used in my worship." And even to this day the sweet scented screwpine flower, on account of this curse of Shiva, is never used in Shiva temples for his worship. And as Brahma lied before Shiva he was cursed to go without temples in this earth. So even now Brahma has no temple in the whole of India. Thus in short runs the legend.

The Krittika feast is celebrated to commemorate the occasion of Shiva's having stood up as a fire-pillar on this day. What the Dipavali is to the Gujaratis in the Gujaratipet of Madras, so is Krittika to the other Hindus. A row of lights will be observed in front of every house on this night in the whole of Southern India. Children take to bursting crackers. The noon-Brahman population of Madras wear new clothes on this day. As Shiva is supposed to have appeared in the form of a pillar of radiance on this day, in every place where there is a Shiva temple a big rod some 25 or 30 feet high is planted opposite to the temple in an open space and left covered up with a thick coating of dried palm leaves from top to bottom. The whole work assumes the form of a leafy cylinder of about five feet in diameter. In the evening, after sun-set, the Shiva god of the village or town is taken out of the temple in a procession. Which procession stops before the cylinder. A brief ceremonial worship is performed and then lighted camphor is thrown at the foot of the cylinder. The whole work now blazes up and a great conflagration ensues which, of course, is so well arranged as not to injure any house or property.

While this cylinder continues to burn, the worshippers assembled there throw pulverised resin over it. This is the closing of the feast in temples situated in the plains. As soon as the leafy pillar is reduced to ashes, the assembled villagers collect the embers which are considered to be the body of Shiva, and miracnlous powers are attributed to them. Sometimes they are used for manuring the fields in the expectation of a good harvest. In the places sacred to Shiva, where temples are situated on the tops of mountains, the burning of the leafy pillar takes place a day after that observed in the plains. Sometimes a big cauldron containing ghee, camphor and other combustibles is lighted on the mountain top and this continues to burn for a whole month. At Tiruvannamalai, Tiruchirapalli, Tiruttani, Mayilam, and other places where the temples are situated on hills, the whole rock on which the pagoda stands is illuminated and the sight is rendered as grand as temple funds will allow. The view at Tiruvannamalai on the Krittika feast night is supposed to be the grandest in Southern India. This feast takes place in the month of Krittika (November-December) when the constellation of that name is in conjunction with the moon, which occurs on the full-moon day of this month. What *Shah-e-Berat* is to Muhammadans so is Krittika to the Hindus-a night of illuminations and lights. This feast is generally supposed to conclude a course of heavy rains that follow the North-east Monsoon. "After Krittika there is no rain" is the Tamil proverb - "*Karttikaikkappuram malai il/ai.*" As in the Dipavali, there are special presents in the

56

Krittika feast also to the newly married bride in the form of clothes, vessels, brass or bronze lamps, and other articles.

# The Mahamakha

The full-moon day of the month of Kumbha (corresponding to 12th February to 12th March) is held sacred by the Hindus throughout India for bathing in the sacred tank called the Mahamakha-saras in Kumbakonam. This occasion, which occurs annually, is called the *Makham, i.e.,* the occasion when the moon passes through the asterism of *Makham* in the month of *Kumbha.* But the *Mahamakham* or the great *Makham* is an event which occurs only once in twelve years. The planet Jupiter takes twelve years to complete one revolution round the sun and during this course when it is in conjunction with the moon in the *Makha* asterism of the constellation Leo-*Simha*-the *Mahamakham* occurs. This is an astronomical incident which takes place only once in twelve years, and when it takes place the event is celebrated as above mentioned. All the holy rivers and bathing places on the seashore are resorted to on this occasion; but the Hindu who takes his bath in the holy waters of the *Mahamakham* tank at Kumbakonam is considered to have reaped the beneficial effects of several baths

in all the holy waters of India. Such being the belief of the
Hindus, an account of the origin of the *Mahamakham* festival
may be interesting. The *Mahamakham* tank, which is biggest
one in Kumbakonam, is situated in the south-eastern portion
of the town and is about a mile to the west of the South Indian
Railway Station there. It is in the shape of a nine-sided polygon
with five re-entrant angles. Two very old Shiva temples
dedicated to Abhimukteswara and Visvanatha are situated
respectively on its eastern and northern sides, and streets run
on the other two sides. The legend of the tank, as disclosed by
the *Sthalapurana* of Kumbakonam, runs as follows:- Under
the orders of Shiva, Brahma collected the essence of the the
sacred waters in the world in a pot and mixed with it nectar
*(devamrita)*. He most carefully secured this pot on the top of
the mountain Meru. But during the great deluge, when the
world was destroyed by an great flood, the pot somehow lost
its position and was observed floating on the water. At the
end of the deluge, when the waters subsided, the pot rested in
a place now called Kumbakonam and at the spot where the
temple of Kumbheswara-from whom the town derives its name
- is situated. The compound word "Kumbakonam," which is
the name of the city, comes from two simple Sanskrit words
*Kumbha* meaning an earthen pot and *ghona* the nostril or
neck of it. Thus the name of the city is conncetcted with the
pot of Brahma. But to continue the legend:- When at the
beginning of the creation of the world after the deluge, the
god Shiva was wandering over the earth in the disguise of a
hunter, he saw this earthen pot, and as he then held a bow in

his hand, he aimed, in sportive mood, at the neck of the pot. The pot broke and the holy water in it began to flow out. It found its level in a hollow pit. This is the very same pit that has become now, according to the legend, the sacred tank of *Mahamakhasaras* at Kumbakonam. When Shiva saw the pot break, he made a *lingam* out of sand and placed it over the pot and infused his own fiery energy into it. When this was doone, Brahma came down from the upper regions with thirty-three crores of *devas* and worshipped the *lingam* in befitting style. He was engaged in his prayers for a very long time, and proceeded to bathe in the tank before him. But lo! a most holy congregation was before him. The great gods Nageswara, Mukteswara and others, the goddesses of all the holy waters of the world-Ganga, Yamuna, Setu, etc., were already waiting there to bathe in the tank along with the lord of creation-Brahma. Even the deity of Benares - Visveswara - had come there not to lose the rare opportunity. They all greeted Brahma and praised him for his faith in Shiva. Brahma proceeded to bathe in the tank by way of bringing the period of his contemplation to a close, and all the gods followed suit and took their baths. These events occurred on a *Mahamakham* day, and from that time forward bathing in this tank on the Mahamakham occasion has come to be considered as equal to bathing in all the sacred rivers and before all the gods. Such then is, according to the legend, the origin of the tank and of this festival.

Every orthodox Hindu believes that the holy waters of the Ganges come down to this tank on this occasion. Most of the old Brahmans say that they observed the goddess Ganga raise one of her hands from underneath the surface of the water of this sacred tank to announce to the anxious pilgrims her arrival in the tank, and that soon after, a lime fruit, a garland of flowers and a roll of palm leaf were seen floating on the water. The latter are considered to be the signs of the visit of a deity, especially of a female deity. The preliminaries to this festival commence ten days before the *Mahamakham* day. From distant quarters of India pilgrims flock to Kumba-koman in very large numbers. On the *Mahamakham* day all the principal idols of Shiva in the town march in procession to this tank. Thousands of pilgrims and devotees follow these idols chanting hymns in praise of the holy rivers. When the procession reaches the pillar post near the Nageswara temple one great mass of moving heads is observed from that elevated position as far as the eyes can reach to the east, south, north and west. For *Mahamakham* is considered the greatest occasion in India, and large crowds flock to witness it. The municipal authorities take the precaution of reducing the depth of the water in the tank and leavle only water just sufficient to enable the pilgrims to bathe without danger of being drowned. This wise precaution has been taken from time immemorial; but instead of the steam engines now used, piccotahs or country water-lifts were used in those old days. The idols of gods that march in procession are temporarily accommodated in the *mandapams* on the banks of the tank. The trident which is the emblem of Shiva is taken out by the priest of each god and immersed in water. This is the signal that that particular god to whom the trident belongs has himself performed the bathing ceremony in the tank. this is also the signal that the holy occasion for the bathing of the people has set in. The twelve tridents are immersed simultaneously in twelve different spots of the tank, and along with these, thosands of devotees plunge their heads into the waters with the firm belief that they are bathing in the quintessence of all the sacred rivers, and in the presence of all the gods. Every one gets up from the bath with his whole body besmeared with mud, but for all that, he goes home with the consolation that the holy occasion has been availed of and that the holy bathing in all the sacred rivers has been taken in one plunge. Such is faith, simple faith, more consoling than all philosophy. What Jerusalem is to the Christians, what Buddha-Gaya is to the Buddhists, what Mecca is to the Muhammadans, what Benares is to the Indian-so is the *Mahamakham* bath to all the Hindus on the *Mahamakham* day. As the water in this tank is supposed to have originated first from the earthen pot so carefully guarded by Brahma, this tank goes also by the name of *Brahma-tirtham*. Owing to the special sanctity attached to it on this occasion, the tank is also called the *Mahamakhasaras*. It is also called *Kaniatirtham* after the goddesses - *Kanyas* - on the tank. These *Kanyas* or virgins are supposed to be the representations of nine holy waters:- *Ganga, Yamuna, Narmada, Saraswati, Godavari, Krishna, Kaveri, Tambraparni,* and *Kanyakumari.* The bath in the *Mahamakham* tank on this sacred occasion is considered to wipe off all sins. The river Ganges is supposed to run into the *Mahamakham* tank by a subterranean current,

63

*Antarvahini,* on this day and the Hindu devotee will assert that if on this sacred occasion the water in the Ganges is examined it will be noticed to have gone down by one foot. Where did the waters go? Of course to the *Mahamakham* tank! How did they go? By the-*Antarvahini*-under current. In connection with this strong belief the following story is related.

In the good old days, before the Kaliyuga had set in, there was a very pious king reigning over the country of Mithila, north of Benares. He was happy in every way except that he had not a son to succeed to his throne. Once upon a time a holy sage, a *rishi,* visited the king and told him that if he bathed in the waters of the sacred Ganges on the *Mahamakham* day he would soon obtain a son. The king had the greatest respect for the sage and desired to follow his advice. He proclaimed his intention among his subjects, and several of these, who were unhappy like the king in not having sons, followed their sovereign. Each started with his wife also; for the Hindu belief is that bathing in holy waters is not complete unless both the husband and the wife hold each the other's hand and bathe together in the waters facing the current. So on that *Mahamakham* day before the Kaliyuga several thousands of families bathed thus in the Ganges with the king of Mithila. All got out of the water safe, except the king and his queen. What became of the royal pair, no one knew. A very careful search was made. The river was dragged with nets. Not the slightest clue could be had; it was a perfect mystery to every one. The loyal subjects returned to their homes with dismal faces and regarded the event as a great calamity.

But the fact was that the king with his queen got out safe from the waters. But instead of meeting with their own people, they met others speaking strange tongues. For the royal pair got out of their bathing at Kumbakonam and not at Benares where they had plunged themselves in the Ganges, because the subterranean current of the Ganges had carried the pair to the *Mahmakham* tank at Kumbakonam. The royal pair had travelled the long distance in the twinkling of an eye. With difficulty they explained themselves to the people at Kumbakonam and found out the real state of affairs. The king's desire has already been fulfilled; for he had a boy. Such is the story and it is very interesting as it is proof positive to the pious devotee that subterranean communication between the Ganges and the *Mahamakham* tank exists even to-day.

The sacredness of grand rivers generally is a strong Hindu belief and the special sanctity attributed to certain waters on an occasion occurring only once in twelve years is an equally strong belief. *Pushkaram* is the *Mahamakham* of the Telugus, and occurs only once in twelve years, when the freshes of the Godavari rise to a very high level. Bathing on the *Pushkaram* day at certain chosen spots on the banks of the Godavari is considered as sacred by the Telugus as the *Mahamakham* bath is by all Hindus.

# The Mahashivaratri

I t is the name of a Hindu festival observed in honour of Shiva, one of the gods of the Hindu Trinity. This falls generally in the month of Magha and the festival is called the *Mahashivaratri* as it is observed on the night preceding the new moon. Not only the night but also the day preceding the new moon in that month is devoted by the Smarta sect of the Hindus to Shiva's worship. On this day the

orthodox Hindu rises early in the morning, bathes and attends most devoutly to his prayers. He attends a temple if there is one nearby. Fasting, as a general rule, is observed throughout the day and night. Sitting up in wakefulness throughout the night entirely absorbed in worshipping Shiva is considered most meritorious. There are special prayers for each of the four watches *(Jamas*-three hours' duration) of the night, and the devotee who goes through these prayers on the night sacred to Shiva is considered to be working his way up to oneness with Shiva after his death.

The *Shivaratri* is also held sacred for the making of holy ashes by the Smartas. Holy ashes are a daily necessity to this class of Hindus, and those prepared on the day sacred to Shiva are considered to be very pure. The process is extremely simple. There are certain days in the year which are held sacred for drying up cow-dung balls, from which holy ashes are made. The balls thus prepared are taken to an open yard of the house on the *Shivaratri* night and placed in the midst of a large heap of husk or chaff. The master of the house or the household priest, who had been observing a fast and repeating prayers the whole day, sets fire to this heap in the early part of the *Shivaratri* night. The heap continues in flames throughout the night and is reduced to ashes the next morning. The latter is then collected and preserved as holy ashes for use till the next *Shivaratri*.

The origin of the sacredness of the *Shivaratri* is related in the following Puranic legend. In a forest, unknown to the public, on the Himalaya mountains there once lived a hunter with his wife and an only child in a humble cottage. He was in the habit of going out daily in the morning with his bow and arrows and returning home in the evening with some game or other which furnished the food for the whole family. As usual he went out in search of game on a certain morning. It was an unusually hot day and he wandered throughout the forest, but was not able to secure any game. The evening was fast approaching. Darkness had almost set in. Thinking it was no use lingering longer in the dense forest he turned his course towards his cottage with a melancholy countenance, for, what could his wife and child do for their supper that night? This was his sole thought. Sometimes he would stop on the way and say to himself that there was no use in going home without any flesh to cook. He saw a big tank on the way, "Ah! to be sure some animal or other must come to this tank to drink water. I shall hide myself behind some thick bush and wait for the occasion." On second thoughts, he considered it safer to climb a tree to be beyond the reach of any beast of prey. To attract beasts to the side of the tree on which he was resting he kept dropping tender leaves from the tree. He was not disappointed in his manoeuvres. During the first watch of the night a doe antelope, after drinking water in the tank, approached the tree to feed of the tempting leaves without any idea of the danger that hung overhead. The hunter, glad at heart, hastily prepared to take aim at the poor beast. The antelope perceived the danger and instead of running away, most piteously addressed the hunter in a human voice, "O!

Hunter dear!Do not kill me now." The hunter, though startled to hear the animal speak in a human voice, said, mustering up his courage: "My charming antelope! I cannot but kill you at once. My wife and child are dying at home from hunger. You must be their food tonight." "Even so, hunter, I have a dear husband and an affectionate child at home. I must take leave of them before I fall down dead by your shaft. For their sake save me for only a few hours. You are not a hard-hearted bachelor. As you feel for you wife and child, surely you must realise what my misery will be if I do not take leave of my lord and child before I lay down my life." The hunter, moved at the piteous words of the beast, thought within himself how hard-hearted he was to resolve to kill a beast so that he may feed on its carcass. But kill he must, if he should eke out his livelihood in that forest. The antelope promised to return after taking leave of her husband and her child. He permitted her to do so and she promised to be back in the fourth watch of the night.

The first watch of the night was almost over. Our hero was wide awake. Having lost his first opportunity that night, he waited for another beast to approach his tree. And his heart leapt with joy at the sight of another beast approaching the tree during the second watch. He again prepared himself to aim his shaft at it. He was again astonished when he heard that antelope also begging him in human voice. Again there was a conversation, in the course of which the hunter learnt that the second antelope was the husband of the first one. It also requested the hunter to spare it till the fourth watch of the night, as it wanted to see its wife and child. The hunter gladly granted the request; for he was sure of carrying away both these beasts at the fourth watch. He thought that beasts which argued in such an honest fashion would never prove untrue. During the third watch appeared the child of the first two antelopes. This beast also astonished the hunter by a similar request, which of course was readily granted, to be spared till the fourth watch of the night.

Thus the three watches of the night were spent by the hunter in strict wakefulness. He had not had even a wink of sleep. The tree on which he lodged for the night happened to be the *Bilva* tree *(crataeva religiosa)* the leaves of which are held to be sacred to Shiva; and in dropping the leaves he was unwittingly offering worship to Shiva throughout the night, for the leaves happened to fall on a ruined image of Siva which lay under the branches of that tree. To add to the hunter's fortune, the night on which all these things took place happened to be a *Shivaratri* night, though the hunter was ignorant of it. The three watches were over. The hunter was anxiously waiting for the return of the three anteplopes as promised. The fourth watch also was running out fast. Still the beasts never came back. The hunter had almost set himself down for a fool for having let the animals go in the first instance. The morning twilight had almost appeared; he turned his face towards the east and a most heart-rending sight met his eyes. There he saw in the dawn of the early morning the three honest animals each weeping at the fate of the other two, unmindful of its own. Even the hunter's hard heart melted away at what he saw. He turned to the other side to hide his tears; but he saw there his wife and child, who after spending the whole night in the forest in his search came running towards him in joy when they saw him. He turned his eyes againtowards the east with something in his mind more noble and elevated than he had ever had. He had almost resolved to excuse the beasts and give back their lives though they had not returned to him yet. But just as the lord of the day was making his appearance on the horizon, there stood before the hunter a divine *vimana* which carried away all the six-the three antelopes, the hunter, his wife and child-to the heavens, to the realm of Shiva. In connection with this marvellous passing away to heaven of the beasts, the hunter and his family, is held the popular belief that *Mrgasira*-the fifth lunar mansion containing three stars in Orion and figured by an antelope's head, which appear in the heavens is a symbolic representation of this Puranic story.

# The Arddhodaya and the Mahodaya

The Hindus regard the two occasions of *Arddhodaya* and *Mahodaya* as very sacred occasions for taking baths in holy rivers and in sacred spots on the seashore. The *Arddhodaya* is considerd to be the more sacred of the two. It is the rising of the sun and the moon in conjunction, at the beginning of which the sun is in Capricorn-*Makara*-on a Sunday in the month of *Pushya* (January-February) and the moon in the 22nd asterism-*Sravana* and the seventh *Yoga*. These five events do not occur in conjunction oftener than once in sixty years. The most important circumstance in the *Arddhodaya* is the half-rising of the sun with which are connected the four events mentioned above. Owing to this half-rising of the sun this occasion is called the *Arddhodaya*, which is a Sanskrit compound meaning the half-rising. Thus the Arddhodaya is a very rare opportunity for sacred baths and we have no recollection of its occurrence in the immediate past.

But the *Mahodaya* occurs oftener. It is considered a little less meritorious as compared with the *Arddhodaya*, but for all that it is also considered a very sacred opportunity for baths. The *Mahodaya* is the rising of the sun and the moon in conjunction on a Monday, the sun being in Capricorn, in the month of *Pushya* (January-February) and the moon in the asterism of Sravana when it is in conjunction with *Vyatipata yoga*. The last *Mahodayas* occurred on Monday, the 5th February, 1894, and on the 1st February, 1895. Both the *Arddhodaya* and the *Mahodaya* are deemed to be very sacred occasions for religious bathing, almsgiving, propitiating the spirits of the departed forefathers, and performing other religious duties. Wealthy Hindus generally go on pilgrimage to bathe in the sacred waters in these places. The sacred water of *Dhanushkoti* near Rameswaram is considered to be most holy on this occasion as it is said to have been opened by Rama with his bow. The Hindus of Madras generally proceed to Mahabalipuram-the Seven Pagodas-to bathe in the sea on this occasion.

Mahodayaam at Mahabalipur

The small village of Mahabalipuram assumes an unusually busy appearance at the *Mahodayam,*a special New Moon day occuring on a Monday in the month of *Pushya*. This special New Moon day occurs once in 30years and as such is considered extremely sacred by the Hindus. Pilgrimages are undertaken to Benares and Rameswaram for baths in the holy Ganges or in the *Dhanushkoti*. Orthodox Hindus who have not the time and convenience for such undertakings, go to some sacred place situated on the sea: and Mahabalipuram on the Madras Coast is a specially sacred place for occasions like this. From the previous Sunday country carts begin to pour in from all directions notwithstanding the difficulties of the marshes on all the sides of this little village. More than a thousand carts could be seen in this place, and boats from the Adyar would be emptying pilgrim-passengers here in several hundreds every hour. The petty traders of Madras make a good profit in selling fruits and other petty things. On the morning of the Monday, more than fifteen thousand heads are seen bathing in the sea. The whole shore would be one mass of Hindus and most fortunately there are generally no accidents of any kind. Mahabalipuram is known to the European world by the antiquarian remains in which the village is rich and which have been well described to the public by many eminent writers on antiquities. All the pilgrim sojourners visit these remains after the bath and the ideas they express of what they see are very amusing and give us an insight into their knowledge of their own history. "These are the caves where the Pandavas lived," say some. "No," denies another with all the authority of a historian and states that these caves were constructed by Rishis. A third greyhead, with anger in his face, states that Mahabali was a very powerful sovereign, that even gods from the heavens were visiting him every day, and it was to accommodate them that Mahabali built these caves. These and such like are the theories. But not one is to be seen expressing a wish to know anything historically about these relics. No one studies or attempts to study them, though several works exist already giving as much as inquiry has hitherto been able to ascertain of information on this subject. Whether these caves accommodated the gods at the time of Mahabali or not, it cannot be denied that they now accommodate the pilgrim sojourners of Mahabalipuram. Thousands and thousands of people find their home now in these Pallava caves. This village is very small and house accommodation is very scanty, the number of ruined houses and those now in occupation being not more than eighty. And where could the fifteen thousand pilgrims find their home for a day now but in thes caves? The whole place is full of people, the major portion being Vaishnavas, by which sect this place is held specially sacred. The bath and sightseeing of the relics are generally over by about ten in the morning and the pilgrims return home for breakfasr. Fortunately a good supply of provisions is kept ready by the merchants. But the supply of pure water is not sufficient, and this difficulty is not felt as the sojourners are all to return to their respective homes by the evening. Visitors from Madras generally go down to Mahabalipuran by the canal and return by the land route *via* Tirukkalukkunram and Chingleput. There is no road between Mahabalipuram and Tirukkalukkunram. There is a rough path by the thick copse of shrub wood in which the plain a round Mahabalipuram abounds, and a walk through it by the setting sun repays all the pain and trouble of a day's sojourn at Mahabalipuram. The fine breeze, the rosy rays of the setting sun, the scenery of the blue flowers of the *Kasan* shrub, the fluttering peacock which happens to be peculiar to this copse, and the sweet scent of a thousand wild flowers cheer the exhausted pilgrim and when the sun sets, the heart of the pilgrim droops down with the approaching night. To add to his gloom the copse changes into marsh and broken country tracks with ruts and muddy pools-till Tirukkalukkunram is reached. Thence it is a nice road to Chingleput, which is covered in two hours by a `jutka' (horse-cart).

# The Mukkoti or Vaikunta Ekadasi

The word *Ekadasi* means the eleventh day of a fortnight, and there are thus two *Ekadasis* every month. All the twentyfour *Ekadasis* throughout the year are sacred to a Hindu. Strict fasting and prayer have to be observed throughout the *Ekadasi* day. The orthodox Hindu bathes early in the morning in a running stream, tank, or well, and goes through a series of prayers. 'He must not hold any conversation with persons of low caste, with those who have renounced the Hindu religion, with liars, with thieves and others of abandoned character. The company of those who are in the habit of plundering the property of others or temple property must be strictly avoided on the *Ekadasi* day. The orthodox Hindu observing this fast must raise his eyes towards the sun to expiate the sin of having seen these bad people, if ever he happens to meet them on this day. He should spend his time in worshipping Govinda with flowers, fruits, incense and Vedic Hymns. He must avoid bad or cruel words in talking to people. He must fast day and night and devote all his time to pure religious thoughts and prayers-all of which must relate only to the god Krishna. *Ekadasi* of the dark half of the month is as pure as that of the light half of the month. He who observes the *Ekadasi* strictly gets all the benefits that are ascribed to the performance of charitable acts during the solar or lunar eclipses or to the performance of the *Asvamedha* or horse-sacrifice. The meritoriousness which is attained by an anchorite after performing penance for full sixty thousand years is acqaired by him who observes but one *Ekadasi*-fast rigidly. The fame which is attained by a donation of 1.000 cows to Brahmans is acquired by him who observes a single *Ekadasi* correctly. The keeping of this fast is more meritorious than the giving of acres as gifts to Brahmans, and more holy than imparting the sacred knowledge of the *Vedas* to students. It is several times superior to feeding starving men, for it is the day most sacred to Vishnu. The observance of this fast on this day gives one eternal felicity in the heavens. The pilgrimage to the holy waters and sacred places is recommended only to those who have not understood the sanctity of the *Ekadasi*. All the hard penances of a rigid anchorite are prompted by utter stupidity inasmuch as he could easily avoid them if he would observe but one *Ekadasi* strictly. He who observes the *Ekadasi* attains all his ends and he who does not observe it is the worst of sinners.'

This is the description given in the *Bhavishyottara-purana* of the sanctity of the *Ekadasi*. Every orthodox Hindu, be he Smarta, Vaishnava or Madhva, has to observe this fast rigidly.

Some of the Vaishnavas and the Madhvas have such a great regard for the *Ekadasi* fasting that they give up on this day the performance of the annual ceremonies to satisfy the *manes* of their departed forefathers if the ceremonies happen to fall on this day. The Smartas and some of the Vaishnavas will consider this as amounting to giving up the ceremonies, inasmuch as they are not performed on the day on which they fall. But those Vaishnavas and the Madhvas who give up the ceremonies have their own arguments for doing so. When they do not themselves eat on the *Ekadasi* day, the *manes* of their forefathers have no claim to be fed by ceremonies and so the right to perform these ceremonies rises only on the day succeeding the fasting day. The observance of the *Ekadasi* day is not solely based upon puranic belief. There are several *Upanishads,* which are regarded to be equal in sacredness to the *Vedas* and which also attribute the greatest sanctity to the observance of the *Ekadasi* fast.

All this is about *Ekadasi* in general. And it must once and for all be said that an orthodox Hindu looks upon all the *Ekadasis* at all times of the year as the same, as far as their sanctity is concerned. He does not attribute more sacredness to one and less to another. But the Vaishnavas consider the *Mukkoti* or *Vaikuntha Ekadasi* the most holy of all the *Ekadasis.* No direct authority for this belief so far as we know exists anywhere in the sacred writings of the Hindus. The *Puranas* and the *Upanishads* speak of the sacredness of *Ekadasi* in general and on this head all are agreed. But what is the reason for attributing special sanctity to the *Mukkoti*

*Ekadasi* which occurs in December-January? The following seems to be the explanation:-Krishna in the *Bhagavadgita* says to Arjuna that if he-the deity-is looked at in the light of months, he is the month of *Margasira* (12th December-11th January). The idea is that this month is more to the liking of the God. As the Mukkoti Ekadasi falls in the light half of this month it must have been held specially sacred by the Brahmans. This sacred day of the light fortnight of *Margasira*, this *Mukkoti Ekadasi*, is represented as a female deity in the *Brahmandapurana* (the gender of *Ekadasi* is feminine) and is said to have originated from the body of Krishna himself. The statement of Krishna in the Gita that he is the month of *Margasira* among months and the story in the *Brahmandapurana* that the goddess presiding over this *Ekadasi* sprung from the body of Krishna himself must be the main reasons for the *Mukkoti Ekadasi* being held highly sacred by the Hindus. Apart from both these, there is another cause why the Vaishnavas deem this day most sacred. One of their great sages, Nammalwar, attained his felicity- *Vaikuntha*-on this day, according to Vaishnava legends. The thirty-three crores of gods are said to have come down to witness it. Hence this *Ekadasi* is called *Vaikuntha Ekadasi or Mukkoti Ekadasi,* which latter is a shortened form of *Muppattu Mukkoti Ekadasi.*

In Vishnu temples, a special gateway leading to the shrine is opened on this day and he who passes through this doorway is considered to have passed through the gates of *Vaikuntha* or the abode of felicity in the heavens, like Nammalwar, a famous Vaishnava saint. The Madhvas and the Smartas who observe the *Ekadasi* equally with the Vaishnavas do not appear to attach any special merit for the passage through this special gateway, which is called the *Vaikuntha* Gateway.

The *Mukkoti Ekadasi* is observed in all Vaishnava temples. Ten days before and ten days after it are also held sacred by the Vaishnava sect of the Tenkalai class, as the recitation of *Tiruvaymoli-* the Tamil *Vaishnava Veda-* is supposed to have taken place before the god Ranganatha in Srirangam on these days. In this sacred island-shrine of the Vaishnavas this feast is celebrated in grand style and pilgrims flock to it from all parts of India.

# The Hindu New Year's Day

Every nation in the world has its New Year's Day. A year is the time of the apparent revolution of the sun through the ecliptic; and a sidereal year is the time in which the sun, departing from any fixed star, returns to the same. The Hindu's astronomical year is sidereal. He calls it *Samratsaradi,* the first day of the year or the *Vishu-Chaitravishu,* the equinoctical point of Aries, into which the sun enters at the vernal equinox. This event generally falls on the 12th April and is considered by the Hindu a *Punaykala-* or a holy occasion. So on the new Year's day the *Manes* and Gods are propitiated by offerings of *tarpana-*oblations of water-and other allied ceremonies. In other respects, the New Year's Day is a day of feasting.

Though the astronomical Hindu year falls on the 12th April, the New year's day is observed on different days by different sects of the Hindus, according to whether they follow the lunar, the luni-solar or the solar calendar. The Tamils follow the solar, and their year is thus the sideral year. The Telugus and the Kannadigas follow the *Chandramana* reckoning, and their year is the lunisolar, which begins earlier than the 12th April. The Malyayalis follow the Tamils, though their *Kollamandu-* which is more an agricultural year-begins about the middle of Sepetmber, when the sun enters the autumnal equinox.

On the New Day the elderly people-males and females-take a sacred bath in the holy rivers or the sea, whichever happens to be nearest. The males propitiate the *Manes* and the deities; children appear in their holday dress and jewels. The nearest temple is attended and the god in it is worshipped. In some families children and other members receive new clothes. A sumptuous meal is cooked in every house and poor relatives are always cordially invited to the feast. At evening time the *Panchanga* or the Calendar of the New year is read out and expounded by a holy Brahman. Several people assemble to listen to this exposition. At the end of this ceremony, *attar, pan supari,* and sweets are distributed. Sometimes a short entertainment of music is also added to this ceremony. The whole day is spent more or less in mirth and festivity and a light supper closes the day's proceedings.

In Malabar, The New Year's Day festivities are observed on a very grand scale. On New Year's eve all the gold coins available in the house, all gold jewels, all kinds of auspicious fruits and flowers and everything considered to be good to look at are placed in the room set apart for the worship of the family god. The Karnavan who is the head of the family first opens this room between 4 and 5 on New Year's morn and worships with a lighted lamp in his hand all these articles. Then every member of the house one after the other goes to the front of the room with his or her eyes shut and opens them at the proper spot to take a glimpse of the auspicious articles collected. The Karnavan-head of the family-presents each with something or other,-coins, jewels, flowers, fruits, etc. This is the chief difference between the Malayalis and other Hindus as regards the observance of the New Year's festivities. And every Hindu whether he is a Malayali or other Hindu takes care to see an auspicious sight on the New Year's morn.

# Kalakshepas-Old and New

One of the striking ways in which Hindu Revivalism has made itself particularly visible, specially among the Hindu community in Madras, in recent years, is the weekly gatherings in different parts of the city to hear religious discourses by professional preachers. These discourses are known as *Kalakshepas?* The word is a Sanskrit compound formed of two simple words meaning "the whiling away of time" The history of the word can be traced to the early days of the earliest of the puranas.

In the good old times of Ancient India, whenever a king or any great personage celebrated a religious sacrifice, several learned persons from remote parts of the country came, on invitation, to take part in the celebration, their primary duty being to assist in the religious rites. And these rites extended over a large space of time, in some instances to as many as twelve years and in some to as few as twelve days. But the majority of sacred rites lasted for a period of twelve months; and the spots chosen for such celebrations were the banks of a stream or river with beautiful groves and natural scenery. The ceremonies connected with the performance of the rites were invariably completed in the first half of the day, and the royal host had to provide some sort of diversion for the guests during the other half. And this diversion had, from early times, been called *Kalakshepa*. The guests, among whom were hundreds of men learned in various branches of study, often had new and old ideas to communicate to and exchange with each other. The sages of old utilised the occasion of such unique gatherings not merely for the pleasant whiling away of their time but, more particularly, for the instruction and mutual enlightenment of the guests. After the midday meal, these learned men assembled under the cool and refreshing shades of the spacious trees of the hermitage and spent their time in the most pleasant and useful manner possible. A few who were learned in philosophy would form themselves into a group under a stately banyan and discuss the several systems of their special branch of study. Another group under the sacred pipal probably codifiers like Manu - would discuss the revisions and amendments of moral and ethical codes. A third batch would be clearing their doubts regarding their intonation in the chanting of Vedic hymns. Thus, according to their tastes and inclinations, the learned sages grouped themselves into batches and carried on discussions in their lines of thought; and, at the end of the period of the sacrifice, they left the hermitage not only enriched by the liberal gifts of the host but with increased knowledge acquired from exchange of thoughts with their fellow-professors, which knowledge they diffused among the people at large during their travels from place to place.

Such gatherings, which in the old days may be said to have somewhat corresponded to the latter day *British Association* stripped of all modern environments, were the result of the ancient form of *Kalakshepa.* And students of oriental literature will find descriptions of such gatherings in the pages of the ancient epics of India, such as the *Mahabharata* and the *Ramayana.* Nay, the whole of the *Mahabharata* is said to have been related during one of these long sacrifices. In ancient times *Kalakshepas* were few and far between. But wherever and whenever such events took place, they always resulted in a substantial addition to the literature of the country and the enlightenment of the people at large.

But now these *Kalakshepas* have multiplied like mushrooms and in many cases persons, with no pretensions to learning, stand up as preachers. The original object of instruction is lost sight of, and Mammon is the God presiding over most of these exhibitions. Most of the *Bhagavatas* are self-styled; and having managed to get a smattering of a few puranic tales, they make *Kalakshepa* of these tales, not on religious occasions but invariably during the *Rahukala* time of a Sunday evening, nor before learned assemblies always, as in days of old, but often before unlearned and uncritical audiences. In the majority of instances today, it is the inspiring nature of the themes chosen for *Kalakshepa* and the accompaniment of music that attract large crowds to such discourses more than the learning or powers of exposition of the preacher. Whether the audiences return home the wiser for having attended such lectures or not, there can be no doubt that the *Bhagavatas* return the richer; for their fees, in most cases, for a lecture range from Rs. 10 to 100 according to their power to amuse, instruct or divert the audiences. One with a decidedly musical talent is more popular among the people than one with mere learning. Sometimes these modern *Bhagavatas* drive in coaches to their places of preaching while the sages of the old had perhaps to perform their long and tedious journeys on foot. Some of them robe themselves in silks and shawls and glitter in diamonds, while the *Bhagavatas* of old were content perhaps with the bark of trees. Many of the popular *Bhagavatas* have only a show of knowledge and are yet admired by an audience who wonder "how such a small head could carry so much wonderful knowledge" in Tamil, Telugu, Kannada, Sanskrit, Marathi, Hindustani, and sometimes English as well. As is the *Bhagavata,* so is the audience.

But in these days of widespread irreverence and irreligion, preachers, however poor in attainments and however low they may have fallen from the standard of the ideal preachers of old, still have some power of God in their hands, provided the Hindu public who are catered for by these professionals learn to be discriminating in the bestowal of their patronage and exacting in their judgment of the qualifications and capabilities of the preachers. There are many religious organizations in

Madras, which ought to combine for their common good and resolve to encourage only the really learned among these professionals. A great responsibility therefore lies on the leaders of the Hindu community in this matter, and, if only they introduce wholesome reforms in their field of popular education a great deal of good might in time be expected by the people.

# Onam

Colourful Onam is the main festival of Kerala. It is celebrated in the Malayalam month of Chingam (August-September) on the Thiruvonam day: This festival heralds the end of the South-West Monsoon, when nature is lush green in her vegetation and adorned in all her floral beauty. Onam is also a harvest festival, coming as it does at the end of the harvest season when people are in a jubilant mood.

The origin of Onam can be traced to the puranas, like the Bhagavata Purana, Vamana Purana and so on. Bali or Mahabali was the king of Kerala. During his reign the kingdom enjoyed peace and prosperity. This Asura or demon-king defeated Indra and conquered the heavens. Bali was a devout worshipper of Vishnu. The gods went to Vishnu for help. To help Indra, Vishnu was born to Aditi the mother of Indra with Prajapati Kashyapa as his father. Vishnu was born as a Vamana in the sixth incarnation of Vishnu.

Bali was extremely proud and conscious of his generosity.

He held a *yajna* and none was refused his request. Vishnu in the guise of Vamana, appeared, to put an end to the might of Bali. Sukracharya, the guru or spiritual guide of the Asuras already knew that Vamana was none other than Vishnu. He personally warned Bali not to fulfil even the least request of Vamana. Bali welcomed Vamana to his *yajnasala* and requested him to ask anything from him as a sacrificial gift. Thus Bali ignored the warning of Sukracharya. Vamana asked for a piece of land which he could cover with his three steps. Bali generously agreed.

As soon as Bali poured the sacrificial water into the hands of Vamana, the dwarf turned into a colossus. His first step covered the heavens. The second step covered the whole earth and his body the intervening space. There was no space left for the third step. Thrivikrama (Lord of Three strides) placed his third step on Bali's head and sent him down to Pataloka (the nether regions). This interesting legend is depicted at the Suchindram temple in Kerala in the most artistic manner.

It is said that at Bali's request Vamana gave him the necessary permission to come once a year to meet his people. On the eve of Thiruvonam, the 2nd and most important day of Onam, Bali comes to meet his people. On this occasion the picturesque state of Kerala gives a symbolic welcome to their king, Bali. Houses are cleaned and decorated with flowers and lights. A fabulous display of fireworks turns the capital Thiruvananthapuram into a veritable fairyland. Sumptuous feasts are prepared. The eldest member of each family presents clothes to all the members of the household. The image of Vamana or Vairochana is installed in each house. Vamana is worshipped in the temple of Tiruvellikkara. He is shown here with his foot on Bali's head. This temple is the centre for the Onam celebrations.

It is at Onam that the formal boat races are held in Kerala. One can finds boats of different shapes. The most popular boat races are held at Kottayam, Champakulam and Aranmula. Huge, graceful boats are rowed by about a hundred oarsmen. The songs sung are typical in character as the rhythm of drums and the clash of cymbals vibrate from each boat. The boats are adorned with scarlet and green silk umbrellas. The number of umberllas shows the affluence of the family. Gold tassels and coins can be seen hanging from the umbrellas. People come from far and near to watch the boat race. It is a also major tourist attraction.

The festival of Onam is celebrated with special emphasis in different places. At Shoranur, Kathakali dancers in gorgeous costumes enact the legends. A strikingly impressive procession of caparisoned elephants is taken out at Trichur.

It is presumed that Mahabali was most probably a Dravidian king, cherished by his people. Mahabalipuram, also known as Mamallapuram was in all probability, his capital or the main port of his kingdom. It may be that he was conquered by the Indo-Aryans. The sociological factor behind the legend may be the fact that the Aryans defeated the non-Aryans and subjugated them. Then they gave the non-Arayn king permission to come to meet his own people. Onam generates income as it is a major tourist attraction and thus helps the economy of the state. It is a festival observed all over Kerala.

# Pongal Sankranti

In South India, the biggest festival of the Hindus is the Pongal Sankranti. Pongal is celebrated after the winter solstice (Makara Sankranti) in the month of Paus (January-February). It is celebrated mainly in Tamil Nadu, Andhra Pradesh and Karnataka. In Tamil Nadu it is known as Pongal and in Andhra Pradesh as Sankranti. Pongal is a sweet preparation of rice, milk and jaggery. So far as Pongal is concerned, the many legends associated with the Hindu festivals are surprisingly lacking. It is a harvest festival and the date coincides with the harvest season. This time marks the end of the North-East Monsoon.

Pongal is celebrated for three days. A 'rath-yatra' procession is taken out from the Kandaswamy temple in Madras on the day of Pongal. The first day of celebrating Pongal is known as Bhogi Pongal. The celebrations are confined within families and it is a family festival. The second day is Surya Pongal or sun worship. Rice boiled in milk and flavoured with jaggery is offered to the Sun God. It is customary for friends to greet each other with the customary question: "Is it boiled?" followed by the reply "Yes, it is". On the third day, cattle (Mattu) are worshipped and the day is called Mattu Pongal. The cattle are bathed and cleaned. Their horns are oiled and beautifully polished. Beautiful flower garlands are hung around their necks. All cattle, animals and birds are fed. Pongal is offered to local deities.

In Tanjore, Madurai and Tiruchirapalli, Pongal is known as Jellikattu. Bundles of notes are tied to the horns of ferocious bulls. Unarmed young men from villages try to wrest the bundles of money. This is the season for new crops. The pulling of the bull reveals the predominance of agriculture in Indian society. This is a harvest festival for farmers. There is a remarkable resemblance to the harvest festival or Paus Parbon celebrated in Bengal.

Pongal is celebrated cutting across social barriers. Community meals are prepared from the freshly harvested rice. Everyone is invited to the meal, rich, poor and even strangers.

# Raksha Bandhan ... (Rakhi)

Raksha Bandhan falls on the full-moon day (Purnima) of the month of Shravan (July-August). Therefore it is also called Rakhi Purnima. The main celebrations of Rakhi Purnima take different forms in different regions.

In the West, the festival is called Nardi Purnima or Coconut Full Moon. To the Hindus, the coconut is of great religious significance. The three eyes of the coconut represent the three eyes of the Lord Shiva. The coconut plays a significant role in Hindu festivals. Coconuts are offered to the God of Water in the presence of a huge congregation on the beach at Bombay.

The festival is also called Saluno, a deviation from the Persian word 'Sal-i-nu' which means the New Year. This ritual strengthens the bond of love between brothers and sisters. Rakhi is also tied on the wrists of close friends and neighbours. Women tie a Rakhi (rosette) around the right wrist of their brothers. If the brother is in a distant place the Rakhi may be sent by post. Women receive gifts and cash from brothers.

Raksha Bandhan has a historical background. About 3000 B.C. Aryans entered India through the North-Western passes and settled in North-Western India. They brought with them their traditional custom, Raksha Bandhan. It was a tradition among the Aryans to have a 'Yajna' before a war to invoke God's blessing for protection and security. Apart from the regular army, the clan leader called on the able-bodied men of the villages to join the war. Before the men departed for the battle field the women-folk tied an anointed sacred thread or amulet:- i) to protect the man ii) to remind him to uphold the honour of his clan. This is how the custom of Raksha Bandhan originated. The word 'Raksha' means protection. Later, different ethnic tribes entered India, each with its own traditional customs. This led to a fusion of Aryan and Non-Aryan customs. Consequently new and modified forms of the various customs came to be. The same happened with Raksha Bandhan.

In the Middle Ages, especially in Rajasthan, it was practised both for imperial alliance and matrimonial alliance. We get innumerable examples of offering Rakhi for such alliances in Todd's 'Annals of Rajasthan'. Marwar was attacked by the Sultan of Malwah. Queen. Karna Devi, the dowager queen of Marwar sent a Rakhi to the Moghul Emperor Humayun, to accept her as his sister and to come to her aid. Humayun responded to her gesture. He drove the Sultan of Malwah away from Marwar and saved the queen. That particular day of Purnima was celebrated as Raksha Bandhan in Marwar and then all over Rajasthan and, finally, throughout India.

Gradully a deeper religious aspect entered this festival. Of the three Hindu Gods-Brahma, Vishnu and Maheswar, the Vishnu cult is said to have been derived from the Aryans. This cult was the most popular of the three, specially because Vishnu represented peace and stability. A variety of regional literature and practices developed around the Vishnu cult. Raksha Bandhan stood for security, stability and fraternity. It was associated with the cult of universal love and brotherhood. In the North and West of India, Raksha Bandhan became a regular feature of society. It celebrated love and brotherhood along with the customary celebration of the divine activities of Radha and Krishna.

Raksha Bandhan was not prevalent in Eastern India. In 1905, Curzon partitioned Bengal on communal lines. A great movement was initiated to oppose the partition. Rabindranath Tagore was one of the prominent figures who vehemently opposed this atrocious partition. In 1905, he introduced the custom of Raksha Bandhan among the Hindus and Muslims of Bengal to nurture an atmosphere of universal brotherhood. This custom became so popular that it spread to every corner of Bengal. It took a very different connotation in Bengal and became a symbol for forging unity between Hindus and Muslims. It also helped to arouse national consciousness against the divide-and-rule policy of the British. Such was the force of the protest that in 1911, the partition of Bengal was annulled. The capital was shifted from Calcutta to Delhi.

Raksha Bandhan has unfortunately degenerated into a cheap, commercial practice where the very essence of Raksha Bandhan is absent and unknown. Sadly, the idea with which it was started -which was to foster love, friendship and universal brotherhood among all communities - is now relegated to the past.

# Rath Yatra Festival

The Rath Yatra festival is held in the month of Asadh (June-July). It is the most unique and complex example of the cultural anthropology of Indian festivals. The *rath* or chariot has been in use since ancient times all over the world. In India, the Rig Veda tells us about Indra and his Pushpak Rath. During the reign of Chandragupta II, of the Gupta Dynasty, the Rath Yatra was held on Buddha Purnima. This has been recorded

by the Chinese traveller Fa Hien. The image of the Buddha was placed on a rath and taken around the streets of the city. It is not improbable that the Buddhist Rath Yatra influenced the Rath Yatra of yesteryears. In far away China, it was customary to carry the statue of Buddha on a chariot. The Burmese Pagoda resembles the Rath temple. Some scholars believe that the temple of Jagannath at Puri was once a Buddhist shrine. In fact, all the major temples of Orissa were Buddhist shrines. They were later converted into Hindu temples. The three images of Jagannath, Balabhadra and Subhadra are modified forms of the symbols of the three Jewels of Buddhism namely, Buddha, the Law, and the Sangha. It is said that the tooth of Buddha is hidden in the wooden image of Jagannath and is replaced into the new image at the time of Nabakalebar.

Mythological background:- After the death of Krishna, his cremation was not performed in the capital of the Yadav royal family at Dwarka. His brother-in-law Arjun, sent his body to Srikshetra (Puri) for cremation. Before the body was totally burnt, his funeral pyre was extinguished by the oncoming waves. The unburnt parts of the body were collected by members of the Sabar tribe. Bishwabasu, the Sabar king, began the worship of the pieces in the dense forest. King Indradhumna stole the remnants of the burnt body. On the instructions of Vishnu, he arranged to insert the charred remains in an image made of neem wood (margosa). He requested Vishwakarma, the God of architecture, to make the image. Vishwakarma agreed to make the image on one condition. If anyone saw him at work, he would immediately abandon his work. As the work progressed, King Indradhumna, driven by curiosity entered the workshop. Vishwakarma, who had already inserted the bits, left at once without completing the limbs. The king prayed to Brahma, who gave eyes, sight and life to the image.

Another version, regarding the origin of Jagannath is connected to the Sabar tribe. In ancient times they worshipped Neelmadhav in the form of a blue stone. Later this took the form of a wooden image. Vishwakarma installed the charred remains of the body of Krishna in the wooden image of Neelmadhav, worshipped by Basu Sabar, a forest tribal king. This image had no limbs. Later King Indradhumna worshipped this as Jagannath. Even now, the local tribals of Orissa who claim to be descendants of the Sabars, play an important role in the worship of Jagannath and are known as Daitas (receivers).

Balaram was considered the God of wine like the Roman god Bacchus. Once, when drunk, he tried to force himself on Jamuna. When she resisted, he dragged her alongwith his plough. Eventually, Jamuna turned into a beautiful woman and satisfied his lust.

The word 'Yatra' has its own connotation. It is a journey. Gundicha was the wife of King Indradhumna. Jagannath visits her house for seven days with Balaram and Subhadra. Her house is the Mausi house with stress on the 'mausi'. The men who receive the images are strangely called Gopinis.

In ancient times Sabar tribals worshipped three deities or Kitungo (main spirit). They were Rambhar Kitungo, Bimba Kitungo and Sitaboi Kitungo. Later the Bramanical cult assimilated these three deities and we have Jagannath, Balaram and Subhadra.

Anthropological aspect:- These popular legends portray certain ancient cults. Firstly, life can be infused into a new image by inserting the remains of the bones of the dead. Secondly, since the images were made of wood, plant life automatically, passed on into the images. Thirdly, Jagannath was most probably some tribal God of the Sabars. These Daitas loved by Jagannath are acknowledged as relatives of the Gods.

Before the Nabakalebar or new image is made, the Sabars or Daitas observe a period of mourning for the death of the old image of Jagannath. When the new image is constructed, (once in every three years) the Sabars have the exclusive right to enter the sanctum. All this undoubtedly points to the fact that Jagannath was basically a primitive God of the aborigines. He has all the characteristics of the ancient totem speak since it is made of just a single piece of wood with no limbs.

We find the existence of this type of totem figure among the aborigines in all parts of the world like the Red Indians or the Gondah, Muriah tribes in Central India. It has been suggested by anthropologists and psychologists that the figure of Jagannath denotes the phallic symbol.

In the days of yore, the fertility and phallic cult were in vogue among the Romans (Bacchus and Saturn) Maypole in

Britain and Flower Day in France. The European tribes such as Slavs, teutons, Cels and Gauls, the South American Salies and Yaghan tribes all worship totems which are composed of one single piece.

Jagannath is the symbol of the fertility cult. According to the Puranas, Balaram is supposed to be the step-brother of Krishna. He is always shown with a plough, the symbol of agriculture. This festival is held at a time when the monsoon is in full swing. It is most necessary for agriculture. Subhadra is a later addition. Reference to Subhadra are found in the Epic Age (in the Mahabharat). She is the sister of Krishna and the wife of Arjun. He abducts her with the connivance of Krishna. This Puranic episode of their going in the *rath* leads to the Rath Yatra and the worship of these three.

Man-woman relationship is signified by the twin deities since pre-historic times. We have Radha-Krishna, Ram-Sita, Lakshmi-Narayan or mother and son like Parvati-Ganesh or two sisters like Lakshmi-Saraswati or even two brothers like Kartik-Ganesh. This is the first and last instance of the worship of two brothers and one sister.

The Puri temple was built by the most powerful king of Orissa, Raja Chorgangadev. It is the assemblage of five chariots or *raths*. The three images were installed between (1112-1140). Jagannath temple is one of the four Dhams of the Hindus. The other Dhams are Dwarka in the west, Badrinath in the north and Rameswaram in the south.

Rath Yatra centres around Jagannath, the 9th incarnation

of Vishnu. Together with him are worshipped his brother Balaram or Balabhadra and his sister Subhadra. The three deities of Lord Jagannath, Balabhadra and Subhadra are brought out of their twelfth century abode, for their annual sojourn to the Gundicha temple in a procession known as the Rath Yatra festival.

The images are made of wood and this takes place at certain times through a festival known as Nabakalebar. The wood for the images has to satisfy certain specific conditions. Certain bits are taken out of the old images and placed in the new ones. The priest who performs the ritual is blindfolded so that he cannot see. His hands are wrapped with cloth and hence he cannot feel. On Jaistha Purnima, the images are placed on a platform and washed with 108 pitchers of holy water to the accompaniment of the chanting of Vedic prayers, the beating of drums and music. They are then repainted by the Daitas and dressed in gorgeous clothes. This ritual takes about 15 days. Then Follows the Rath Yatra.

This festival attracts people from all over the world. The deities are taken out from their temple on Nilachal mountain in Puri through the Lion Gate. they are placed on three resplendent chariots on multiple wheels numbering 43, 32 and 16 respectively. Jagannath's *rath* is called Nandighosh. It is 45 feet high and painted yellow. Balaram or Balabhadra's chariot is known as Teladhwaja. It is blue in colour and 44feet high. Devi-rath or Darpadolana is 43 feet high and belongs to Subhadra. The king of Puri then pays homage to the deities and sweeps the chariots. Hundreds of thousands of fervent devotees crowd the Baadanda, the road leading to the Gundicha Mandir. All wait anxiosly to pull the chariot and catch a glimpse of the Lord. It is believed that anyone who pulls the rope will find salvation. A 'darshan' or vision of the Lord is called 'Adap' darshan. After 7 days the deities are taken back from Gundicha Mandir to their own temple.

This is the most important festival of Orissa. It breaks across barriers of caste, creed and religion. Jagannath or Purushottam symbolises the integration of people from all walks of life and all corners of the country. Rath Yatra is a major tourist attraction. It helps to boost the state's economy as numerous industries have developed around this festival.

It was Vaishnavism with its precepts of love and social equality that gave this festival its present colour. This happened in the 16th century with the ascent of Sri Chaitanya in the religious world. The Rath Yatra of Orissa is a totally different from that in Bengal. The Rath Yatra festival came into Bengal in the wake of Vaishnavism, with certian changes. According to mythological heresy, a clandestine relationship between Jagannath and Subhadra is hinted at, particularly in Orissa. When pulling the chariots, snide comments are made about Jagannath and Subhadra.

Bengal:- The Rath Yatra festival of Mahesh in the Serampore area of the Hoogly district is second only to that of Puri. This festival is about 500 years old. The shrine of Lord Jagannath was founded by Dhrubananda Brahmachari at the end of the 15th century. Erosion of the Hoogly led to the abandonment of the original temple site. The present temple was built by Nayanchand Mullick of Calcutta in 1775. The chariot of Jagannath was presented in 1885 by Krishna Chandra Basu. The four-tier iron chariot draws thousands of people. A mela or fair with temporary stalls is set up.

The Iskcon Rath Yatra at Mayapur is a venue vibrant with people coming from all corners of the globe. This festival is also held in Varanasi and all over Gujarat.

# Hindu Funeral Rites

A Hindu funeral, as it is now performed, has undergone many changes from what it was originally meant to be by the ancient sages of India, and as such deserves handling in a critical way. Every religion has its own mode of conducting its funeral rites. The Hindu mode is that the son or the sons or the nearest kindred must perform these parting ceremonies. As soon as all hope of life is given up, the family priest summons all the sons to sit by the side of the dying father. To avoid confusion, let us suppose the dying party to be the father, and that his sons perform the rites. Certain donations are first given to the Brahmans. A lighted lamp, a vessel full of sesamum seed, a vessel filled with oil, a milch cow with its calf-these four must be given, or if a person is too poor to buy a cow, he must at least give a couple of rupees. These donation are considered to be most effective in washing away the sins of the dying man; and, as a corollary, he who receives the gifts is supposed to inherit the sins of the dying person. Hence it is very difficult to find persons to receive the donations voluntarily; and to induce the acceptance of them, large fees have sometimes to be offered. The men who accept the bribes are Brahmans of very inferior social scale, who appear with hideous faces, which proclaim that the average lustre of their caste has left them long ago. Then follows the sacred bath to purify the soul and atone for the sins of the dying person - it is called the *Kaveri or samudra snana,* as the person dying happens to be near a river or the sea and fees are paid to Brahmans, who are supposed to perform the ablutions. The fee for each bath is generally six annas and a quarter. In rich families fees are given for a thousand such baths. As it is considered very respectable to receive this kind of fee, a good number of high class Brahmans is always available for this purpose.

After giving the gifts enumerated above, the son or sons of the dying man sit near his head and chant hymns from the *Vedas* to the dictation of the family priest. This is a most solemn occasion. The weeping and crying and other outward manifestations of mourning cease. the purport of the prayer is that all the sins of the dying man may be absolved and that he may find a happy abode in Heaven. When the dying man actually expires, the prayer ceases and all the relations go into the street mourning and wailing, facing the south-this amounts to an appeal to the God of Death - whose quarters are supposed to be in that direction-to show mercy to their dead relative. Then the whole household assembles round the dead person, and incessant weeping and wailing proceed for three or four hours. The males, however, do not give vent to their sorrow in .

this way, and generally keep themselves aloof. Some of the old-women chant mourning ditties which they repeat and make a pretence of weeping. If any of these old women have any insinuation to make, they take this opportunity of making them, and quarrels spring naturally, after the mourning days are over. When the time for the removal of the corpse to the burning ground arrives, the body has be washed and decorated. The religious rites for the preparation of the sacred fire to ignite the funeral pyre have to be performed near the corpse. The daughters and other close female relatives of the dead man bring water in pots and wash and decorate the body, while the sons perform the religious ceremony and prepare the sacred fire. In the meantime the construction of the bier goes on outside the house. When everything is ready, the leave-taking ceremony takes place. This consists in the dead man's palm being rubbed with as many two-anna pieces as there are close relatives, and these pieces being then presented to those relatives, who keep them as long as they live. When this is concluded, the corpse is placed on a bier of green palm leaves, the grandsons standing ready with lighted torches to accompany the bier to the burning ground. Young women stay at home but elderly ones always accompany the corpse. At the burning ground, elaborate religious ceremonies are gone through, at the end of which large a fee along with food is paid to religious Brahmans. These relatives are the fathers or fathers-in-law (or the nearest male relatives in that direction) of the sons who perform the funeral rites. If the person who died has seven sons, the duty of supplying the mourning house with food falls on the fathers-in-law of all the married sons. The outside supply of food is necessary for the first, second, tenth, eleventh, twelfth and thirteenth days. If there are six different parties to to undertake this kind of supply, they do it in turns. If their number is insufficient, some of these days are left out and only important days, as the first, tenth and the thirteenth, are chosen, or any one or two of these days. So far as the rule goes, it is a wise provision, for when the house goes into mourning, its comforts in the direction of feeding will be neglected unless some outside relation is chosen for the occasion. This duty of supply is called *sar vaikkiradu,* which means the supplying of food with pepper water; that is simple food as was the rule in ancient days. But the modern Hindu custom is to supply a grand feast with all the trimmings. All kinds of fruits, sweets and varieties of rice-preparations are offered to the mourners. One father-in-law vies with another in his competition to give grander and grander dinners on the successive days, and to crown the horror, quarrels sometimes spring up among some of these idiotic relations that due and proper invitation was not sent to such and such a party to be present at the dinner. Did the sages ever mean that their simple ruling should be thus abused by modern civilisation? The sooner the old and orthodox custom is resumed the better. On the night of the thirteenth day presents in the shape of new clothes, rings and money are given the children of the deceased by their relatives. New clothes die worn by almost all and the mourning proper becomes a thing of the past. The monthly ceremonies are kept up and the annual ceremony closes the career of the dead man in his relationship with the world and, in the world of the dead, he becomes a *mane* or *pitri*.

# Saraswati Puja

**S**araswati Puja is undoubtedly the most popular festival in the eastern region. Saraswati is the goddess of learning, arts and crafts. According to her different specialities she is known by different names like Bakdevi, Biraj, Sarada, Brahmi, Satarupa, Mahasweta, Sarbasukla, Prithudar, Bagiswari and, ofcourse, Saraswati.

This festival is held in the month of Magh (January-February). It is a festival celebrated by the youth, particularly students who invoke the blessings of the goddess for success in learning, arts and crafts. Throughout Bengal Saraswati Puja is celebrated in schools, colleges, clubs as well as homes.

Among all the Hindu deities, Saraswati stands out as the most controversial. Her origin is shrouded in mystery. Starting from the Vedas, Puranas, Upanishads to the popular ancient mythology, Saraswati appears through a veil of mystery.

According to the Matsya Purana, Saraswati evolved from the mouth of Brahma. Such was her beauty and grace that Brahma pursued her. As she fled in different directions a head appeared and so Brahma is attributed with five heads. she was the most unique creation of Brahma. Saraswati is our equivalent of the classical Goddess Minerva and also the Teutonic Goddess Fira. The moon and the lotus associated with Saraswati are both symbols of eternal womanhood.

Some of the many mythological stories connected with Saraswati have interesting sociological interpretations. The gods and the demons by mutual agreement decided to churn the ocean for the Amrit or the elixir of life. Mainak mountain was used as the churning rod and Basuki as the churning rope. when Lakshmi appeared with the Amrit kunbha both wanted the elixir. Saraswati with her exquisite beauty lured away the asuras. As the Gods were drinking the Amrit, Rahu and Ketu, two asuras saw them and slipped in with the Gods. As they drank the Amrit which would make them immortal like the gods, Vishnu detected them. He immediately cut off their heads. The two enraged asuras, swallowed the sun and moon but could not retain them as their throats were cut. This led to the origin of the solar and lunar eclipse. Saraswati, who was instrumental in helping the Gods to be immortal, was established in the heavens as the Goddess Saraswati.

The Gods and the Gandharvas both wanted the Soma Ras. It was again Saraswati who with her beauty and grace lured and so exhausted the Gandharvas that they could not acquire the Soma Ras which naturally went to the gods.

The Aryans fought with the non-Aryan Comi tribes (tribal dominance among the Aryans) like Nished, Sabar and Pulindar on the banks of the river Saraswati. At the request of Vishnu, Saraswati disappeared underground and again re-appeared in far off Rajasthan. The tribals were thus deprived of the life-saving water. They were forced to abandon the area. In both cases we see the importance of the river Saraswati in Aryan life and how Saraswati was used to deprive the weak of water, without which life is impossible. Saraswati is known as Prithudhar (subjugator of the Aryans).

Vashishtha and Vishwamitra, the two sages, were both violently opposed to each other. Vishwamitra ordered the river Saraswati to wash away Vashishtha along with all he possessed. Saraswati refused to comply with his command. To punish Saraswati, he turned the water of the river into blood. At the behest of Shiva, the two sages became amicable and once again there was pure water in the river Saraswati.

In some areas she is believed to be the daughter of the Sun

or Surya Kanya. In Western India, Saraswati is seen with the lion or peacock. She is married to Kartikeya. This is really the sun cult.

In Eastern India, particularly Bengal, Saraswati has been absorbed into the Bengali culture. She has been given the mantle of daughter of Parvati and is treated as a daughter. Vishnu had three wives-Saraswati, Ganga and Lakshmi. He was tired of Saraswati because of her superior knowledge and so gave her away to Brahma. Ganga was too frivolous and so was given to Shiva. Lakshmi quiet and sedate, remained his wife. These were the three Sris.*

History tells us that the Aryans came to India through the Khyber pass and settled in Punjab, Haryana and North Rajasthan. Saraswati is one of the seven holy rivers flowing through modern Punjab, Haryana and North Rajasthan.

* In the North West along the banks of the river Saraswati. They were a pastoral people and the river was their means of communication as well as source of life.

Hence Saraswati was highly venerated and is associated with the fertility cult.

The mythological background of Saraswati shows the importance of the river Saraswati in the life of the Aryans settled along her river banks. Sociologically the River Saraswati was an important factor in ancient civilization. She is therefore a part of the fertility cult.

The Aryans who lived along the banks of the river were

pastoral and rural.

All early development took place on the river bank. Consequently Saraswati came to be venerated as a symbol of knowledge.

It is evident that the upper strata of society used their superior knowledge and expertise to deprive the ignorant lower half of society.

The other name of Saraswati is Prithudhara. It has an important sociological aspect. The Comi tribes were subdued by being deprived of the most essential requirement, water. This story influenced Tagore to write Muktadhara (a play) where Bibhuti the engineer uses his superior knowledge to deprive the ignorant farmers by constructing a dam to divert the river water and satisfy the king.

* The story of Kalidas has been built around Saraswati. There was a proud and learned princess who rejected all suitors who could not match her knowledge. The pundits in anger planned to marry her off to a fool. They saw a man cutting the branch on which he was sitting and decided he was the ideal fool for the princess. Kalidas was presented to the princess as a man of wisdom who only spoke in signs. The pundits answered all the princess's questions by interpreting Kalidas's signs. The two were married but on the wedding night the princess realized she had been duped. She kicked Kalidas out of her bed. He in sorrow and shame went to commit suicide. The Goddess Saraswati appeared and asked him to take a dip in the river. As he emerged from the river Kalidas was

transformed. He began to recite verses in praise of the Goddess. Unfortunately for him he began to praise her beauty not from her feet upwards but from her breasts downwards. Saraswati in anger cursed Kalidas for his audacity. He would die in an ignonimous place.

This festival is celebrated all over Bengal with great fervour and gaiety.

# The Kaliyuga

We are enabled to place before our readers to-day* an admirable article on the Kaliyuga from the pen of a learned Hindu gentleman. The word "Kaliyuga" is constantly cropping up in native writings and speeches, and is likely to do so still more in the furture, but a perusal of this article will explain the belief, for a superstition it cannot fairly be called, based as it is on writings held sacred by the people. That extraordinary divine, Dr. Cumming, used to startle periodically worthy British matrons and susceptible young men and maidens by proving to his and their complete satisfaction that the end of the world was near at hand. His prophecies were the result of abstruse mathematical calculations based on his interpretation of certain scriptural texts; but, so far as we are aware, he never brought forward such strong evidence as is furnished in the Puranic writings which fixes the exact hour of the dawn of the Last Day at 2 A.M. on the 25th November, 1899. The point, however, on which particular stress is to be laid is the difficulty that must naturally exist in dealing with people who honestly believe in this Kaliyuga story during such a crisis as the present. Even the most sceptical will read with some surprise of the evils accompanying the close of this age as described in the *Vishnu Purana*. They tally so closely with recent changes in the social order of Hindu life. [Editor, *The Madras Mail*.]

A Yuga in Sanskrit (in Heb. *Olim,* in Gr. *Aion,* and in Lat.*AEvum)* means an age of the world. Four *Yugas* are recognised by the Hindu mythology, the *Krita,* the *Treta,* the *Dwapara* and the *Kali*. All these four *Yugas* joined together constitute a great age, or an aggregate of four ages*(Mahayuga)*. A thousand such aggregates are a day of Brahma. Let us give the number of years allotted to each *Yuga* in the years of the gods and in the years of men. The first rule is that a year of men is equal to a day of the gods. The following table gives the years of the four *Yugas* according to both these calculations:-

| Yugas. | Divine | years. | Years of Mortals. |
|---|---|---|---|
| Krita ... | | 4,800 | 4,800x360=1,728,000 |
| Treta ... | | 3,600 | 3,600x360=1,296,000 |
| Dvapara ... | | 2,400 | 2,400x360= 864,000 |
| Kali ... | | 1,200 | 1,200x360= 482,000 |
| | | | Total (a Mahayuga) 4,320,000 |

So the notion of these four ages may be best remembered by deteriorating series expressed by a descending arithmetical progression as 4, 3, 2, 1, by the conversion of units into thousands and by the legend that these are divine years each composed of 360 years of men. A period of 4,320,000 years constitutes a great age, or a *Mahayuga,* and this number multiplied by 1,000 i.e., 4,320,000,000 years becomes a day of Brahma:-

*Daivikanam Yuganam tu sahasram parisamkhyaya / Brahman-ekamaharijneyam tavati ratrir-eva cha.* At the end of this day a dissolution of universe will occur, when all the three worlds, earth and the regions of space will all be consumed by fire. The three worlds then become but one mighty ocean. Brahma will sleep for a night, of equal duration with his day, on this ocean and at its close will create the world anew. A year of Brahma is composed of 360 such day and nights and a hundred such years constitute his whole life, which is called a *Kalpa. Brahmanaschayusha Kalpa kalpavidbhih nirupitah.* Such, in brief, is the belief of the Hindus regarding the ages and the duration of the world and full details of this belief will be fould in Books I, IV, V and VI of the *Vishnu Purana.*

What is the object of Brahma in thus destroying the whole universe and recreating it? The Hindu philosophy most beautifully explains it:-

Sarva-bhutani Kaunteya

rakritam yanti mamikam!

Kalpa-kshaye punas-tani

127

Kalpadau visrijamy-aham!!

"I absorb the whole universe in myself at the end of the *Kalpa* and at its commencement I create it again," says Brahma. Volumes are written in the several *Puranas* about the merits and demerits of each *Yuga,* or age. The brief way to remember the whole subject would be to imagine Virtue to have four legs. In the *Treta,* or the second *Yuga,* on only one leg. After this brief remark about the Hindu notions of the age of the universe, its destruction and recreation, let us confine ourselves on the present occasion to the full description of the *Kaliyuga,* the fourth Hindu age which is current now, and in which Virtue is said to walk only on one of her four legs. The *Kaliyuga* era commenced in 3102 B.C. and we are now in the year 4998 years of the *Kaliyuga;* i.e., 4,997 years of the *Kaliyuga* have already passed away and the year current 4998 commenced on the 12th April, 1896. The year 5000 of the *Kaliyuga* will commence on the 12th April 1899, A.D. and end on the 11th April 1900. The belief of the orthodox Hindus from the Himalayas to Kanyakumari is, that this, their fourth, era is one of vice, Wickedness and misery is universal, and is recorded in almost each and every one of their *Puranas.* It is also strongly believed that the year 5000 of the *Kaliyuga* will be a year of doom and ruin. Let us dwell at length on both these beliefs.

In Book IV of the *Vishnu Purana* it is stated that Kali feared to set his feet on this world as long as it was purified by the touch of the sacred feet of Krishna.

Yavat sapada padmabhyam

Sprisan-aste Ramapatih!

Tavat Kalir vai prithivim

Parakrantum na ch-asakat!!

The usual notion of the Hindus is that the age of Kali set in from the death of Krishna; but it is also a common supposition that it commenced a little later, with the reign of Parikshit. It is said in Book II. of the *Bhagavata* that after Krishna died or ascended to his abode in Heaven, the Pandavas also followed him after installing their grandson and heir, Parikshit, as the Emperor of *Bharata*. The new monarch, according to the usual custom, set out on a tour round his empire to establish order, to make friends with friendly kings and to subdue vassals. He finished his tour and was returning to his capital, when, on his way back and near the river Saraswati he noticed that a cow and an ox were being tortured to death by a person who appeared to be a Sudra, and who had put on royal robes. The cruel Sudra had cut off three of the four legs of the ox and was proceeding to cut of the fourth leg also. The cow appeared to be only a bag of bones; she was so lean and dried up by starvation. Even a heart of stone would have melted away at the sight. But the Sudra went on kicking and lashing her incessantly. Parikshit was horrified at what he saw and in great wrath addressed the person as follows:- "Who are you, vile wretch, that have put on royal graments? Are you not ashamed of your conduct towards these poor creatures, one of which you have already deprived of its three legs and the other you have starved to death? I must put you at once to death." The Emperor then asked the ox and the cow to relate their story. After some reluctance the ox said that he was Justice (or Virtue, *Dharma*) who walked on his four legs of (1) contemplation upon God, (2) purity of life, (3) mercy towards living beings, and (4) truth in the *Krit yuga* and that he had only leg, truth, left remaining at the commencement of the Kali era and that lord of the *Kaliyuga* was already aiming at his fourth leg. The Emperor learnt the cow was the goddess Earth who was reduced to that condition by the departure of Krishna from this world of men. Parikshit was horrified at what he saw and heard, and aimed his death-dealing sword at the Sudra, when, wonder of wonders! he threw away his royal garments, assumed his true form and falling down before the Emperor, begged for his life. This Sudra was Kali himself. Parikshit was a true hero and a genuine sprout of the Pandava family. His mottc was never kill a fallen enemy. So he spared Kali's life on condition that he left his dominions at once. But Kali begged for some place to live in. He was asked by the Emperor to find his abode in gambling houses, in taverns, in women of unchaste lives, in slaughtering-places and in gold. And Kali agreed to do so. So, as long as Parikshit reigned over Bharata (India) Kali confined himself only to these five places; but after the reign of that just Emperor, Kali made his way to other places like wild fire and established his power throughout the length and breadth of the whole world. This, in short, is the legend of the setting in of the *Kaliyuga*.

In India, when a young boy or girl happens to break, in eating or dress, the orthodox rules of caste, his or her parents will say: "O! It is all the result of the *Kaliyuga*." If a Hindu becomes a convert to any other religion, or if any atrocious act is committed the Hindu will observe: "O! It is the ripening of Kali." Every deviation from the established custom every vice, every crime, in fact everything wicked, is set down by the ordinary Hindu to the ascending power of the Lord of the Kali age. These notions entertained by the people must not be entirely set down to be wholly superstitious. In every one of the Hindu *Puranas* the *Kaliyuga* (or the dark age) is described as the worst period of everything wrong, unhappy or miserable. The *Vishnu Purana, Bhagavata, Devibhagavata,* and a number of religious works give a glowing description of the numerous miseries reserved for mankind in the *Kaliyuga,* and the ordinary Hindu bred from his infancy in the *Puranic* lore has accepted these beliefs as part and parcel of his existence, and anything going wrong in his ownhousehold or around him is set down to the influence of the Kali age. Parasara describes the evils of *Kaliyuga* in detail in the *Vishnu Purana.* The strict rules of caste, order and observances will never exist. The rights enjoined by the four *Vedas* will perish. The rules of conduct between the husband and wife, between the precepter and his disciple will be disregarded. Marriage rules will be set at naught. Every book will be a sacred book. All gods will be gods. People will turn proud at small possessions. Wives will desert their husbands when the latter become poor and take up with persons who are rich. A person possessing money will be the lord of everything, irrespective of his birth or position in life. All money will be spent on mere show. The world will become avaricious. Men will desire to acquire wealth by dishonest means. Cows will be fed only as long as they supply milk. The people will ever remain in fear of famine and scarcity. They will ever be watching the sky for a drop of rain. Severe famines will rage and people will be driven to the necessity of living upon leaves of trees. There will never be abundance or pleasure in the Kali age. Kings, instead of protecting their subjects, will plunder them under the pretence of levying taxes. Men of all degrees will believe themselves to be equal to the Brahmans. Everyone who happens to have cars, elephants or steeds will fancy himself to be a Rajah. There will be no warriors or Princes who could be called by such names on account of their birth. People will desert their houses. Children will die in great numbers. Women will bear children at the age of 5, 6 or 7 and men beget them when they are 8, 9 or 10. Grey hair will appear when a person is only 12 years of age and the duration of life for men will only be 20 years. The *Vedas,* the gods, the Brahmans, the sacred waters, will all be disregarded. The parents-in-law will be respected in the place of parents and brothers-in-law (brothers of wives) will be one's bosom friends. Sins will be committed daily and everything which brings down misery on human beings will be found to be prevailing to the greatest extent in the Kali age."

This is but a part of the description given in one of the greatest of the Hindu *Puranas* on the evils of the Kali age. The railway carriage where a Brahman and a non-Brahman sit side by side in the same compartment and the schools where English is taught in the same way to a Brahman as to a non-Brahman, instead of exciting the admiration of the orthodox Hindu for the benefits they have conferred upon the public, are looked upon as the platforms where Kali plays most for levelling of caste distinctions. Female education, though authorities exist in the *Puranas* Themselves for such a course, is viewed as another turn which Kali has taken to corrupt womankind. The several Government and Municipal taxes are considered to be the miseries of the mighty reign of Kali without the least consideration that the subject is bound to pay to the State for his own protection. The Hindu mind is ever ingenious in looking upon everything from a Kali point of view. But we must, at the same time, mention here that it is only the Hindu who lives in remote villages and who has not had the advantage of a free education who thinks thus. Every educated Hindu, of course, takes the right view of the case. Thus ends our description of the *Kaliyuga* in general and of the evils thereof as found in the *Puranas* and as prevailing among the people.

In addition to this belief there is yet another, and a strong one, that the year 5000 of the *Kaliyuga* (April 1899-April 1900) will be a year of doom and ruin. The famine that is threatening now a great portion of India, the grain riots everywhere, the failure of monsoons, the Bubonic plague in Bombay, the several fires, and floods in almost all the great rivers *(Mahanadis)* this year, such as the Krishna. Godavari, Kaveri, Narmada and Tapti, which have caused immense loss of lives and property, are believed by the uneducated classes to be ushering us into a period of general cataclysms which is expected to take place in the last days of 1899 A.D. We will examine now the sources of the belief. Although all the *Puranas* are unanimous in describing the miseries of the Kali age there is fortunately only one *Purana* which speaks of the ruin of the world in the year 5000 of the Kali age. But this one *Purana* is the greatest authority to the whole of India. Its name is the *Devibhagavata* and it is regarded as a most sacred book. In the 6th chapter of Book IX it is related that the three goddesses Saraswati, Ganga, and Lakshmi had a quarrel among themselves in heaven and each cursed the other. By the power of the curses they were converted into the rivers of Saraswati, Ganga (Ganges) and Padmavati in this world and are expiating their sins here. Lakshmi in addition to her form as the river Padmavati has assumed also the shape of the shrub *Tulasi (Oscymum sanctum)*. In the 8th chapter it is stated that these goddesses will abandon this world in the year 5000 of the *Kaliyuga* and with the disappearance of these noble rivers everything will disappear from the world with the exception of two places-Benares and Brindavan. The original in Sanskrit stands thus:-

Kalau pancha-sahasram cha

Varsham sthitva cha Bharate!

Jagmus-tas-Hereh padam!!

Vihaya Sir-Hareh padam!! (1)

Yani sarvani tirthani

Kasi Brindavanam vina!

Yasyanti sarvam tabhih cha..

Vaikuntham ajnaya Hareh!! (2)

(1) They-the goddesses Saraswati, Ganga and Lakshmi, after having stayed in this world for 5,000 years of the *Kaliyauga* in the shape of rivers, gave up their transformed shapes and went to the abode of Vishnu (heaven).

(2) All other holy things, too with the exception of Kasi (Benares) and Brindavan (Mathura) accompanied them to the abode of Hari by the order of Hari.

The statement contained in the above two verses is believed to be the highest authority for the impending doom. In the year named excepting Benares and Brindavan, everything holy will disappear from the world. The year 5000 of *Kaliyuga* occurs in two other places also in the *Devibhagavata,* once in the middle of Chapter 7 of Book IX when Narayana pronounces the liberation of the curse to the goddesses:-

Kalau pancha sahasne cha

Gate varshe cha mokshanam!

'When 5,000 years of the Kali age have expired you will be liberated from the curse.' Again in Chapter 13 (1st verse) where Narada asks Narayana to relate to him what happened to the goddesses after the year 5000, he says:-

Kalau pancha-Sahasrabde

135

Samatite Suresvara!

Kva gata sa Mahabhaga

Tanme vyakhyatum arhasi!!

Thus from a minute examination of the *Devibhagavata,* the year 5000 is alluded to in only three places in Chapter 8, 9 and 13 of the ninth book of that work. And it is only in Chapter 8 that the disappearance of everything from the world in the year 5000 *Kaliyuga* is alluded to. And the Hindu belief in the *Puranas* is that everything happens as predicted therein and even so the doom and ruin of the year 5000 will come to pass as foretold by the *Devibhagavata.*

In addition to the Puranic belief there are a few verses current among the astrologers of India which imply that the Hindu religion will perish in the year 5000 of the Kali age. They are as follows:-

Kalau pancha-sahasrante

Vishnuh tyakhyati medinim ! (1)

Yada Vishnur-divam gachchhet

Tada Veda-viparyash !! (2)

Yada Veda-viparyasah

Tada jyotir-divam vrajet ! (3)

Tasmat-tu pancha-sahasram

Phala-sastram Kalau yuge !! (4)

They mean (1) Vishnu abandons this world at the close of

136

the year 5000 of the *Kaliyuga*. (2) When Vishnu goes away, the Vedas will be turned upside down. (3) When the Vedas have suffered thus, the splendour of the planets will vanish. (4) So, the truths of astrology will be current in this world only up to the year 5000 of *Kaliyuga*. These verses, which allude to the ruin of India three years hence, are said to have been uttered by Krishnamisra, a poet who flourished in the Court of Vikramaditya at Ujjain in the 11th Century A.D. These are the only sources for the strong Hindu belief that year 5000 will bring general ruin to the whole world. Some are charitable in stating that if the whole world is not ruined, there will be wonderful changes and utter misery and famine at least in that year. At what time of the year 5000 will this ruin overcome India will be the next question.

In the Hindu calendar every month has a Zodiac called Rasi with the position of the planets for the month indicated in it by astronomical calculations. Generally not more than a single planet will be found in each of the 123houses, or mansions, of the Zodiac. Rarely two or three or even four will be found once in several years in one and the same mansion. But if more than four of the planets are found combined in the same house a great calamity is foreseen. The following verses of the *Jyotisha Sastra* may be read with interest:-

Pancha griha hanti smaste desan

Shashta griha hanti samsta bhupan!

Sapta griha hanti samasta lokan

137

Nirmartyam ashta griha samyutena !!

They mean that the combination of five planets in one of the mansions of the Zodiac in any month will lead to the destruction of all countries; the combination of six planets, to the destruction of all Kings; that of seven, to the destruction of all worlds, and if eight planets combine the universe will be. rendered destitute of men. Bhishma the just and the greatest warrior of the world fell in the wars of the *Mahabharata* in the month of *Magrasira* (December) on the new moon day-*Amavasya*-when seven planets combined in a single mansion of the Zodiac of that month. But for that combination such a mighty warrior would never have fallen. This is the belief of the Hindus. The year 1896 A.D., is, as we have stated already, is 4998 of the *Kaliyuga* corresponding to the year *Durmukhi*of the *Brihaspati* cycle of 60 years. Five thousand *Kaliyuga* will be 1899 A.D. and the year *Vikari* of the *Brihaspati* cycle. According to the astronomical calculations of the Hindus, eight planets meet in the mansion of Scorpio *(Vrichhika)*to the last week of November, 1899, at the 23rd *Ghatika* i.e. 2-6 A.M. on the 13th lunar day (trayodasi) of the dark half of that month. Between that time and the succeeding new moon day, i.e., two days after that combination a great ruin will come over India. India may not be entirely depopulated or devoured by floods, but famine, pestilence, war and other miseries will reign over the whole country. This is the strong belief and November 1899 is the expected time.

How strongly this belief has taken possession of the Hindu mind will become plain to our readers if they refer to the

*Madras Mail* of the 24th October last. It will be found there that an astrologer addressed the Dewan in the Mysore Representative Assembly held in October last to make provision for performing *pujas* (worship) to the planets and to propitiate them to avert the impending catastrophe of the year *Vikari (1899 A.D.)*, Kaliyuga 5000. Some of the members apeared to have been seriously occupied with that matter. The Dewan promised to place the subject before the Maharajah. Eight planets, it is said, according to the astronomical calculations in this country, meet together in November 1899, in the mansion of Scorpio, and not six as the Mysore astrologer stated. Some astrologers say that the meeting of the eight planets is impossible and that only seven meet in one mansion. A Tamil Pandit and astrologer named Mr. Kandaswami Pillai, of Dindigul, in the Madura District, predicted some time ago that the year 1899-Kali 5000-will be one of terrible famine far exceeding that of 1877 in its horrors by reason of the conjunction of the Sun, Mars, Mercury, Venus, Jupiter, Saturn and also the Solar node *(Rahu)* at one and the same sign of the Zodiac Scorpio in November, 1899.

But let us all be more hopeful. The annals of India show a regular series of famines separated by intervals of not more than 3 to 8 years, sometimes 10, and lasting frequently over a year, even as long as three years. The most prolonged famine that India ever experienced was that of 1876-78. The S. W. Monsoon failed in 1875 and 1876. The N. E. Monsson did not bring in sufficient amount of rain in these years. Between 1876-78 people died in thousands. Whatever the uneducated

139

Hindu may say about the horrors of Kali, these famines must be attributed more to the peculiar position of the mountains in India, especially in the Deccan and Southern India. This interferes with the even distribution of rain. We are fortunately at the end of 1896 A.D. Whatever may be the popular belief about the end of the world in November, 1899, let us only suppose that if any calamity at all is ever to happen as predicted by the *Puranas,* that the years 1897-99 will be a period of prolonged famine as that of 1876-78. Fearing that such may be the case, apart from the puranic ideas, the Government and the charitable public, as would now and then be seen from the columns of the *Madras Mail,* are already adopting measures to avert its evils.

The year 5000 of Kali is the turning point of a minor cycle of 5000 years commencing from Krishna. It is believed by the Occultists that spirituality gains ascendancy after 5000 *Kaliyuga.* It is quite natural to expect such extraordinary events to take place during the time of the change of either major or minor cycle.

# *Weekly Gods*

### Ravi-var (Sunday)

This day is influenced by the Sun. Ravi is another name of Surya, the Sun God. He has a red complexion and it is auspicious to wear red on this day. He rides on a chariot with one wheel which is pulled by seven horses. He may have two or four hands which carry two lotus flowers or a conchshell and a disc. Sunday is a good day to start a new endeavor. Usually Ravi is an inauspicious planet in astrology.

### Som-var (Monday)

This day is under the influence of the moon planet (Soma). Soma has a white complexion and carries a mace. He rides on a chariot with three wheels pulled by three horses. It is good to fast and wear white on this day. Someone who is born under the influence of Soma will be respectable, rich, powerful, have many friends, and be honored. This is usually an auspicious sign.

## Mangal-war (Tuesday)

Mangala (Mars) has a red complexion. He has four arms and carries a club and a trident. He usually rides a ram, but also rides in a chariot. A person under the affect to this planet has a tendency to suffer, be accident-prone, to be robbed, attacked or put in prison and to have their good name ruined. This planet is usually detrimental and is often worshiped to get rid of its detrimental effects. One can wear **red** to help with this planet. If a king starts a war on this day he will be victorious. One should not a start an auspicious activity on this day. A copper triangle is his symbol.

## Budh-war (Wednesday)

This is the day of Mercury (Budha) who has a light yellow complexion. He also wears **yellow** clothes and a yellow garland. He has four arms and carries a club, a sword and a shield. Budha's influence is normally neither favorable nor unfavorable. Budha exerts its influence in reference to the other planets. It is considered especially auspicious to feed Brahmins on this day. Soma, the mood god, is his father and Tara is his mother.

## Brihaspati-var (Thursday)

Brihaspati is the priest of the demigods, and he is also called Guruvara. He has four arms and holds beads (a rosary), a club and a ball. He has a golden complexion. He usually sits on a lotus or rides on a chariot pulled by eight horses. The color of Thursday is yellow. Someone under the influence of Brihaspati will have a lot of wealth.

## Shukra-var (Friday)

Shukra is the planet Venus. Shukra means "bright." Shukra is the teacher of the demons and knows how to bring the dead back to life. He has a white complexion. He is seen with four hands, two hands are holding a club and beads (a rosary) and the other two hands may be in the protective or boon giving positions. He is usually seen sitting on a lotus, but sometime may be seen riding on a chariot with a lot of flags that is being pulled by eight horses. A silver square is his symbol.

Shukra is the most auspicious planet. A person under the influence of Shukra will be honored across the land and will attain a high office.

## Shani-var (Saturday)

Shani is the planet Saturn. This planet is potentially is most detrimental. If this planet is wrongly placed in a person's a chart it can cause great misfortune to that person, such as poverty and loss of loved ones. Shani is black colored and is seen with four hands, which may hold a trident, a bow and arrow, or a rosary. One of his hands may be in the gift-bestowing position. He rides either a vulture or in an iron chariot. He is the son of Surya and Chaya.

There are several Shani temples found in temples of other gods throughout India. By worshiping Shani one can rid oneself of the misfortunes that can by caused by this planet. To gain the ultimate benefit this planet should be worshiped on Saturday.

Due to the curse of his wife, Shani can cause destruction by just looking at someone. Therefore he is seen looking down, so as not to cause destruction to anything.

FNTB